Editor
Sara Connolly

Editorial Project Manager
Betsy Morris, Ph.D.

Editor-in-Chief
Sharon Coan, M.S. Ed.

Product Manager
Phil Garcia

Imaging
Alfred Lau

Acknowledgements:
Microsoft® Excel software is
©1991–2003 Microsoft
Corporation. All rights reserved.
Microsoft® Excel is a trademark
of Microsoft Corporation,
registered in the U.S. and other
countries.

Publishers:
Rachelle Cracchiolo, M.S. Ed.
Mary Dupuy Smith, M.S. Ed.

Microsoft™

Excel

for

Terrified Teachers

Authors

Jan Ray, Ed.D.
Karen Wiburg, Ed.D.

Teacher Created Materials, Inc.
6421 Industry Way
Westminster, CA 92683
www.teachercreated.com

ISBN-1-57690-3838-0
©2003 Teacher Created Materials, Inc.
Revised, 2003

Made in U.S.A.

Table of Contents

Table of Contents *(cont.)*

Introduction

Welcome to *Microsoft Excel for Terrified Teachers*. You hold in your hands a book that I hope will soon be tattered and torn from continuous use. So, don't plan to stay terrified of *Microsoft Excel* any longer! I firmly believe that once you see how great *Microsoft Excel's* workbooks are for your own personal and professional productivity that you will naturally want to share them with your students. After all, you're a teacher. Right?

To begin with, I've developed a series of twenty-four **Teacher Activities That Teach** just for you. These activities are designed not only to increase your comfort level and workbook skills but also to help you with your day-to-day duties like calculating grades and scheduling the learning centers in your classroom. There are also activities that go beyond the day-to-day duties—like charting your students' progress. Once you understand the basic concepts and skills that underlie each activity, you can modify the data as necessary to make each workbook truly your own. Bet you can't wait!

Of course, the next big step is to use *Microsoft Excel* as an instructional tool with your students. You will be amazed at how quickly they pick up the workbook skills and concepts you provide. The sixteen student lessons found in the **Student Lessons for Learning** section cover a wide range of content areas and grade levels. From literature to geography, you will find a student lesson that complements your current curriculum. Of course, as a teacher, I know that you have become a master at adaptation. So, feel free to change any of the student lessons to meet your specific classroom needs.

Anxious to get started? Thought so!

A Note About the Screen Displays in This Book

Whenever possible, I have included two sets of screen displays for the steps you take when creating worksheets and charts within the **Teacher Activities That Teach** section. You will also see two screen displays for every worksheet and chart in the **Student Lessons for Learning** section. The first screen displays what you will see when working on a PC (personal computer that is IBM compatible). The second screen displays what you will see when working on a Mac.

What Is Microsoft Excel?

Microsoft Excel is a software application that can be used as a tool for all your "number crunching" tasks and responsibilities. A *Microsoft Excel* worksheet looks like an electronic ledger. After you enter data into the worksheet, the program can perform mathematical calculations at your command, including adding, subtracting, multiplying, and dividing.

Just so you know, *Microsoft Excel* is so powerful, it can instantly perform even more complex computations, such as the "reverse of the one-tailed probability of a chi-squared distribution." But don't worry! Elaborate statistical functions are beyond the scope of this book. Thank goodness!

Microsoft Excel can also create a chart from the data in your worksheet in a flash. All you have to do is decide which type of chart you would like displayed. There are so many to choose from, including column charts, bar charts, line charts, pie charts, area charts, and more. You can make simple changes to column and bar charts to display pictographs. There are even charts for displaying the high, low, and closing rates for all your stock investments.

Well, are you impressed with *Microsoft Excel* so far? Thought so, because I am too. It seems that every day I discover new ways to use *Microsoft Excel* worksheets and charts to help me track and display everything from strength training performance at the YMCA to the projected growth of my retirement plans.

But don't let the power of *Microsoft Excel* intimidate you. You'll be amazed at how easy this software application is to learn and use. So, let's get started.

About the Version of *Microsoft Excel* Used for This Book

It seems that every year or two *Microsoft* comes out with new versions of its software applications, including *Excel*. With each new version come changes in features, functionality, and form. The version of *Excel* used for this book is XP if you are using a PC and X if you are using a Mac. If you are using an older version of *Microsoft Excel*, you may wish to purchase an earlier version of ***Microsoft Excel for Terrified Teachers***.

About the CD In the Back of This Book

Turn to the back of this book and you will find a CD. It contains resource files for the **Teacher Activities That Teach** and the **Student Lessons for Learning**. The CD does not contain the *Microsoft Excel* software application. *Microsoft Excel* must be installed on your computer system prior to using this book and resource CD.

There are several types of files on the CD, including activity files, template files, data organizers, and more. Nearly every teacher activity and student lesson in *Microsoft Excel for Terrified Teachers* has associated CD files. You will find a complete list of these files in the **CD Index** found on pages 303-304.

You will also find copies of all workbook files you will be creating in the **Teacher Activities That Teach** section, beginning with **Activity 4—Saving, Using, and Renaming a Workbook Template**. You can use the workbook activity file to compare the workbook you created with the workbook I created. Also, if an activity asks you to open a workbook file that you haven't created because you skipped an activity or two, you can always use the one on the CD to complete the teacher activity. When it is time to save the workbook activity, be sure to save it on your hard drive, network drive, or floppy diskette. (Since the CD is a CD-ROM [ROM stands for Read Only Memory], you cannot save the changes you make to any file back to the CD.)

You will find template files on the CD as well. Some template files will be created as you complete the **Teacher Activities That Teach**. The template files associated with the **Student Lessons for Learning** are already created for you. They are all on the CD. Template files are meant for you to open and immediately save under another name on your computer system. That way, the original template file always remains intact, ready for you to use again and again. So, if you open a template file, before entering any text or other data, click File on the Menu bar and select Save As. Navigate to where you want to save the file on your computer system. Then click Save. Then you can enter text and other data, knowing that the original file is intact. That's all there is to using a template file!

Many of the student lessons have data organizers, activity sheets, information files, and more. You will find the files you need to conduct the **Student Lessons for Learning** listed under **Materials** at the beginning of each lesson. You will also find a list of all files associated with the **Student Lessons for Learning** under **Related CD Files** at the end of each lesson.

Feel free to create a *Microsoft Excel* **for Terrified Teachers** folder on the hard drive of your computer system. Download all the files from the CD into the folder for your access convenience.

Getting Started

Before starting the *Microsoft Excel* teacher activities and student lessons, you should know how to launch the program, understand some basic *Microsoft Excel* terminology, be able to navigate a worksheet, and know how to close the workbook file and program properly. If you have already mastered all of these skills, feel free to skip ahead to the **Teacher Activities That Teach** or the **Student Lessons for Learning**. You can always check back here if there is something that you are unfamiliar with or have forgotten how to do.

Launching *Microsoft Excel* on a PC

There are several ways to launch or open the *Microsoft Excel* program. Here are the two easiest ways to launch *Excel* on a PC.

First, look on your screen. If you see a *Microsoft Excel* icon, double-click on it to launch the program.

Second, if you don't see a *Microsoft Excel* icon, open *Microsoft Excel* through the Program menu. Click once on the **Start** button on the Task bar. When the Start pop-up menu appears, scroll up to **Programs**. When the Programs menu appears, scroll over to **Microsoft Excel** and click once to select it.

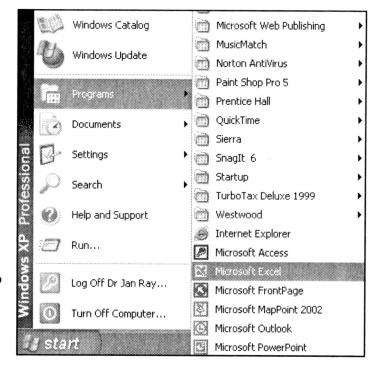

Launching *Microsoft Excel* on a Mac

To launch *Microsoft Excel* on a Mac, double click on the hard-disk drive to open it. Then double click on the *Microsoft Office* folder to open it. Finally, double click on *Microsoft Excel* to launch the program. At the **Project Gallery** dialog box, click the *Excel* **Workbook** icon, if necessary. Then click **OK**.

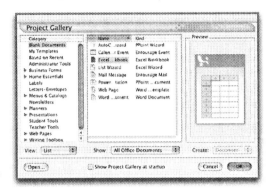

Getting Acquainted with *Microsoft Excel*

Before designing your first worksheet by adding text, numbers, and formulas, take a look at the blank worksheet on your screen to become familiar with its components and unique terminology.

Microsoft Excel Terminology

Notice that the worksheet is a large grid made up of columns, named A, B, C, etc., that run up and down, and rows, named 1, 2, 3, etc., that run across. A, B, C, and so on are called column headings; 1, 2, 3, and so on are called row headings. Cells are the rectangular boxes formed where columns and rows intersect. Each cell within a worksheet has a unique cell address that begins with a letter (to indicate the column), followed by a number (to indicate the row). Move your pointer arrow to the following cell addresses and click the mouse button to select them: **A4**, **F7**, and **C10**.

Notice that when you select a cell, the surrounding gridline changes to a solid, darker line. This new cell border indicates the active cell within a worksheet. Move your pointer arrow to the following cells and click the mouse button to make them the active cells: **B8**, **E12**, and **D4**.

Just above the top left-hand corner of the worksheet, the name box always indicates the address of the active cell or group of cells. As you move your pointer arrow to the following cells and click the mouse button, watch the name box display each cell address: **C3**, **E14**, and **I9**.

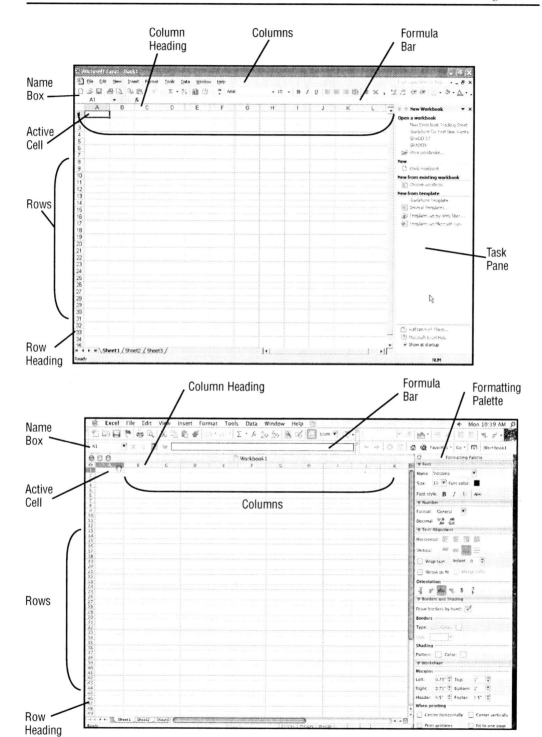

Column Heading

Columns

Formula Bar

Name Box

Active Cell

Rows

Row Heading

Task Pane

Column Heading

Formula Bar

Formatting Palette

Name Box

Active Cell

Columns

Rows

Row Heading

Note: If you are using a Mac, you will not see the name box until you display the formula bar. To do so, click **View** on the Menu bar. Then click **Formula Bar**.

To the right of the name box is the formula bar. Click in cell **D3** and type the year **2003**. Notice that 2003 appears in both the active cell and in the formula bar.

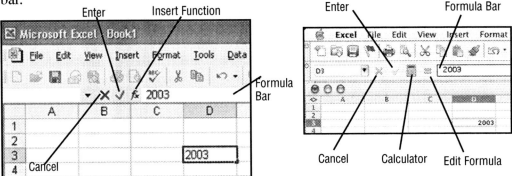

On the PC three small buttons appear to the left of the formula bar once it is activated—the **Cancel** button (**X**), the **Enter** button (**✔**), and the **Insert Function** button (*fx*). Clicking on these buttons enables you to cancel the contents of the cell, accept the contents of the cell, or get help creating a formula, respectively.

On the Mac four small buttons appear to the left of the formula bar once it is activated—the **Cancel** button (**X**), the **Enter** button (**✔**), a **Calculator** button, and an **Edit Formula** button (**=**).

Click the **Enter** button to accept the year 2003.

There are just a few more parts of the worksheet that you should be aware of before proceeding. At the top of your screen, find the title bar that reads *Microsoft Excel* - **Book1** on the PC and **Workbook 1** on the Mac. A file in *Microsoft Excel* is considered a workbook. Each workbook contains several related worksheets. At the bottom of your screen, find the worksheet tabs, named Sheet1, Sheet2, etc. You've been working on Sheet1. Click on the Sheet2 tab to move to the second worksheet. Click on the Sheet3 tab to move to the third worksheet. Then click on the Sheet1 tab to return to the first worksheet. Worksheets can be added, deleted, named, moved, copied, and more. (You'll learn how to do that soon!)

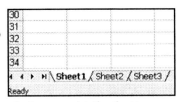

On the PC, in the upper right-hand corner of the screen are the standard Window control buttons. Depending upon your view, the control buttons enable you to minimize, maximize, restore, and close the workbook file, the *Microsoft Excel* program, or both.

On the Mac, the Window control buttons are located on the upper-left corner of the workbook. These buttons allow you to close, minimize, or maximize (or zoom) the file.

Below the title bar are the menu bar, standard toolbar, and formatting toolbar. You are probably familiar with some of the features of these bars from using other *Microsoft Office* applications. Features unique to *Microsoft Excel* worksheets will be integrated throughout the teacher activities.

Note: If you are using a Mac, you will need to display the Standard toolbar and the Formatting toolbar. To do so, click **View** on the Menu bar. Click **Toolbars**. Then click **Standard Toolbar**. Repeat these steps to display the **Formatting Toolbar**.

About the Task Pane

When you open a *Microsoft Excel* workbook in XP for the PC, notice that there is a Task Pane on the right-hand side of your screen. (On a Mac, this is called the Formatting Palette). Although it may seem awkward to you at first, the Task Pane will become a valuable, time-saving tool once you get comfortable using it.

Close Task Pane Button

Sometimes, the Task Pane takes up too much workbook space. When that happens, you can remove the **Task Pane** from your screen by clicking the **Close** button in the upper right-hand corner of the display. (For a Mac, click the **Close** button on the upper left.) By deselecting the **Show at startup** at the bottom of the Task Pane, you can keep it from displaying when you open your *Microsoft Excel* files.

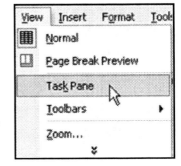

If the Task Pane is not displayed, and you need it for a specific task, such as when you want to save a file as a template, you can always recall it. Simply click **View** on the Menu bar. Then click **Task Pane** (or **Formatting Palette** for the Mac).

Recalling Workbook Terminology

Here's a list of terms you've just been introduced to. Check off those you understand. Review those you don't. How are you doing so far?

- ❏ Active cell
- ❏ Book or workbook
- ❏ Cancel button
- ❏ Cell
- ❏ Cell address
- ❏ Columns

- ❏ Edit formula button
- ❏ Enter button
- ❏ Formatting toolbar
- ❏ Formula Bar
- ❏ Menu bar
- ❏ Name box

- ❏ Rows
- ❏ Standard toolbar
- ❏ Title bar
- ❏ Window control buttons
- ❏ Worksheet

Navigating a *Microsoft Excel* Worksheet

There are several ways to navigate or move around an *Excel* worksheet, including using the mouse, keyboard, menu bar, name box, and scroll bars and boxes. Be sure to practice each of the basic navigation techniques until you feel comfortable using them.

Using the Mouse

When you use the mouse to point and click within a *Microsoft Excel* workbook file, it takes two shapes. Move your mouse over the title bar, the menu bar, and the formatting toolbar. Notice that your mouse takes the shape of a **pointer arrow** when in these areas. Next, move your mouse over the *Microsoft Excel* worksheet grid. Notice that your mouse takes the shape of a **cell pointer**. Clicking around is pretty easy!

Using the Keyboard

You can use the arrow keys (←,→,↑,↓) on your keyboard to move one cell to the left, right, up, or down, respectively. Practice using each arrow key, moving around your worksheet quickly.

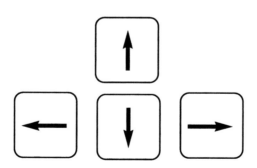

Note: If you have a **<Scroll Lock>** key on your keyboard, you can press it and scroll using the arrow keys without changing the active cell.

Use the **<Tab>** key to move one cell to the right. Use the **<Shift><Tab>** key combination to move one cell to the left.

The **<PgUp>** and **<PgDn>** keys on your keyboard allow you to move up or down one full screen of the worksheet. Try them!

The **<Alt><PgUp>** and **<Alt><PgDn>** key combinations on your keyboard allow you to move one screen width to the right or one screen width to the left on the worksheet.

Note: If you are using a Mac, the Option key is equivalent to the Alt key on a PC.

The **<Ctrl><End>** key combination makes the last cell used in your worksheet the active cell.

The **<Ctrl><Home>** key combination makes cell **A1** the active cell.

Using the Menu Bar

To navigate your worksheet using the menu bar, click the **Edit** menu and select the **Go to** command.

At the Go to window, type the cell address **E14** in the Reference command line. Then click **OK** to make **E14** the active cell.

Using the Name Box

Remember the name box that always displays the address of the active cell? Click in the name box. The existing cell address highlights, waiting to be changed.

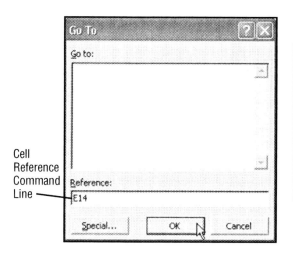

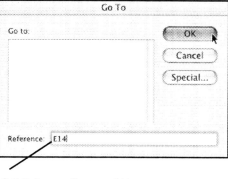

Cell Reference Command Line

Cell Reference Command Line

Simply begin typing a new cell address, such as **G4**, and press the **<Enter>** or **<Return>** key on your keyboard. The address you typed becomes the active cell.

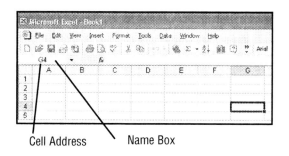

Cell Address   Name Box

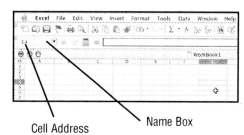

Cell Address   Name Box

Using the Scroll Bars and Boxes

If you want to view another part of your worksheet without changing the active cell, use the vertical and horizontal scroll arrows, scroll bar, and scroll lines. They are located on the right-hand side and bottom of your worksheet window.

Using your mouse, click on the up or down scroll arrows (▲, ▼) to scroll vertically row by row. You can also click and drag the scroll bar (■) up or down. If there's room on the scroll line, click above the scroll bar to move up one page. If there's room on the scroll line, click below the scroll bar to move down one page.

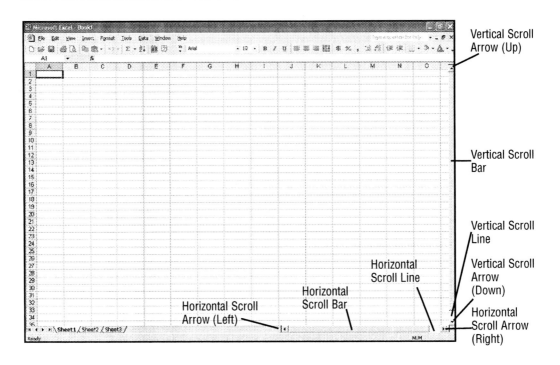

Vertical Scroll Arrow (Up)

Vertical Scroll Bar

Vertical Scroll Line

Horizontal Scroll Line

Vertical Scroll Arrow (Down)

Horizontal Scroll Bar

Horizontal Scroll Arrow (Right)

Horizontal Scroll Arrow (Left)

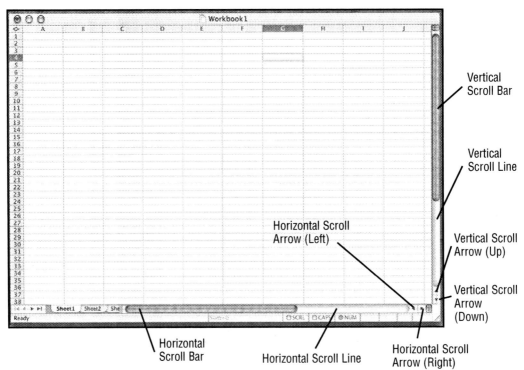

Vertical Scroll Bar

Vertical Scroll Line

Horizontal Scroll Arrow (Left)

Vertical Scroll Arrow (Up)

Vertical Scroll Arrow (Down)

Horizontal Scroll Bar

Horizontal Scroll Line

Horizontal Scroll Arrow (Right)

Using your mouse, click on the left or right scroll arrows (◄ ►) to scroll horizontally column by column. You can also click and drag the scroll bar (■) right or left. If there's room on the scroll line, click to the right of the scroll bar to move one page to the right. If there's room on the scroll line, click to the left of the scroll bar to move one page to the left.

Reviewing Navigation Techniques

See how many of the navigation techniques you can quickly recall and demonstrate. Check off those you understand. Review those you don't.

- ❑ Using the <Alt><PgDn> key combination (<Option><PgDn> on the Mac)
- ❑ Using the <Alt><PgUp> key combination (<Option><PgUp> on the Mac)
- ❑ Using the arrow keys on the keyboard
- ❑ Using the arrow pointer and clicking the mouse
- ❑ Using the <Ctrl><End> key combination
- ❑ Using the <Ctrl><Home> key combination
- ❑ Using the Go to command under the Edit menu
- ❑ Using the horizontal scroll arrows
- ❑ Using the horizontal scroll box
- ❑ Using the vertical scroll arrows
- ❑ Using the vertical scroll box
- ❑ Using the name box to change the cell address
- ❑ Using the <PgDn> key
- ❑ Using the <PgUp> key
- ❑ Using the <ScrLk> and arrow keys
- ❑ Using the <Shift><Tab> key combination
- ❑ Using the <Tab> key

How are you doing so far?

Exiting *Microsoft Excel*

When you are done working in *Microsoft Excel* on the PC, there are two simple ways to close the program.

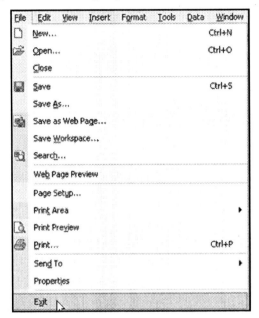

First, you can click **File** on the Menu bar and then select **Exit**. You can also click on the **Close** button or box on the Title bar.

If you are using a Mac, go to the **Excel** menu and select **Quit** *Excel*.

Using either technique, you will be prompted to save your workbook file. Since this workbook was used just for practice, click **No** or **Don't Save**.

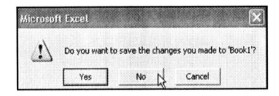

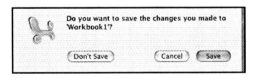

Note: In all future activities, you will be saving your *Microsoft Excel* workbook files before closing the program.

Well, are you ready for some real workbook activities that teach you even more? Great! Go ahead to the next section—**Teacher Activities That Teach**.

Activity 1—Entering Column Labels Using AutoFill

Now that you have the basic vocabulary and navigation techniques "under your belt," it's time to start your first worksheet. Don't worry. There are no numbers or formulas in this worksheet. In creating a **Learning Center Schedule**, you will focus on entering and formatting column and row labels. Ready?

Getting Started

1. Launch *Microsoft Excel* to open a new workbook.

Entering Column Labels Using AutoFill

First you'll enter the days of the week as column labels.

2. Click in cell **B1** and type the column label **Monday**.

Note: Although you may be tempted to type the remaining weekdays in cells C1 through F1, **DON'T**! Let *Microsoft Excel* do it for you by using **AutoFill**, a feature that automatically extends a series, such as days of the week.

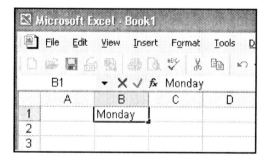 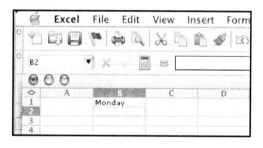

3. Using your mouse, point to the fill handle—the small square at the bottom-right corner of the active cell (B1).

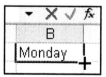

Note: When the cell pointer is positioned on the fill handle, it changes to a black cross on the PC and a box with two arrows on the Mac.

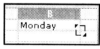

4. Click and drag the fill handle to the right, highlighting cells **C1 through F1.**

5. Release the mouse button. The days Tuesday through Friday automatically appear.

Troubleshooting Tip

If you dragged the fill handle too far and woefully see several more days of the week than required, don't despair! Just stop what you are doing and click **Edit** on the Menu bar and select **Undo**. Voila! Your extended days of the week have disappeared. Take a deep breath and try again. (Just so you know, **Edit/Undo** is one of my favorite and most frequently used commands.)

---

6. Click in any blank cell to remove the highlighting and view the days of the week you entered using the AutoFill feature.

Note: Don't be concerned if the column label *Wednesday* is not entirely displayed. You will learn how to adjust the column width in Activity 3. So, relax and hang in there.

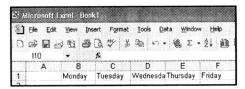 

Entering Row Labels

Next you'll enter the names of the learning centers as row labels. Feel free to substitute the names of the learning centers in your own classroom.

7. Click in cell **A2** and type the following: **Computer Center**

8. Click in cell **A3** and type the following: **Art Center**

9. Click in cell **A4** and type the following: **Science Center**

10. Click in cell **A5** and type the following: **Reading Center**

11. Click in cell **A6** and type the following: **Math Center**

12. Click in cell **A7** and type the following: **Listening Center**

Note: Notice that most of the row labels in Column A appear to extend into Column B. You'll fix all overlapping row labels by adjusting the column widths in Activity 3.

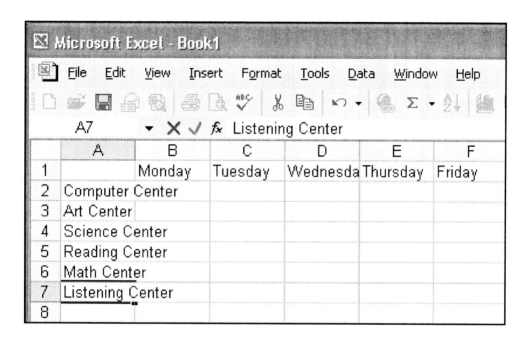

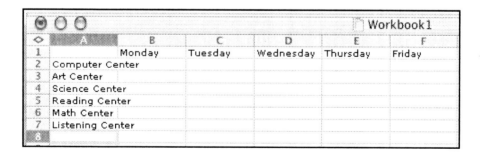

Ready to format those column and row labels? Great!

Activity 2—Formatting Column and Row Labels

In this activity you will format the column and row labels you just entered. Are you ready to learn some new formatting tricks? Thought so!

Formatting Column Labels

1. In order to format the column labels (Monday through Friday), select the row by clicking on the row heading 1. When you do, notice that the entire row highlights, allowing you to apply the following formatting commands to all the column labels at once.

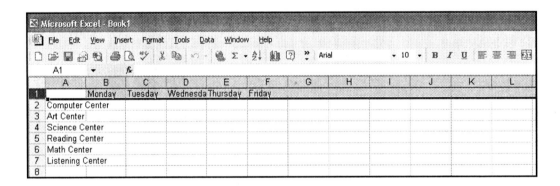

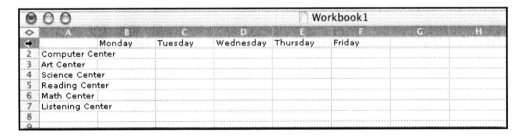

Note: If you are using a Mac, display the Standard and Formatting toolbars, if they do not appear on your screen. Click **View** on the Menu bar. Click **Toolbars**. Select **Standard**. Then repeat these steps, selecting **Formatting**.

2. Click on the **Bold** button (**B**) in the formatting toolbar to bold the days of the week. You can also click on the **Italic** button (**I**) to italicize and **Underline** button (**U**) to underline the days of the week. It's up to you!

Note: I chose to only use the **Bold** command in my worksheet. So, if you used other commands, keep in mind that your worksheet will look a bit different—which is okay.

3. Click on the **Center** align button in the formatting toolbar to center the days of the week.

4. Click on any empty cell in the worksheet to remove the highlighting from row 1 and view the formatting changes made.

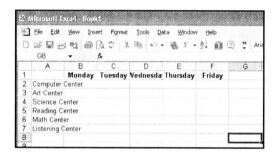
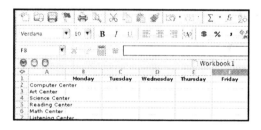

Formatting Row Labels

5. In order to format the row labels (**Computer Center** through **Listening Center**), select the column by clicking on the column heading A. The entire column highlights, allowing you to apply the following formatting commands to the selected cells.

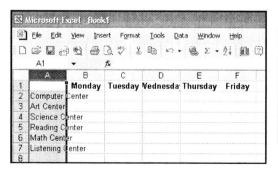
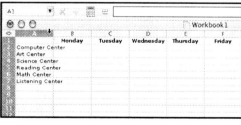

6. Click on the **Bold** button (B) in the formatting toolbar two times to bold the learning centers. (The first click deselects the bold from the column, as cell A1 was already bold from the formatting of the column labels. The second click bolds the entire column.)

7. Click on the **Italic** button (I) to italicize the learning centers.

8. Click on any empty cell in the worksheet to remove the highlighting from column A and view the formatting changes made.

 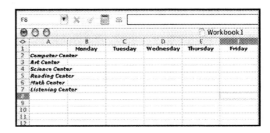

The column and row labels are now formatted. It's time to adjust the column widths so that all the labels fit within their respective cells. Ready?

Activity 3—Adjusting Column Widths

In this activity you will learn how to adjust the column widths in several different ways.

Look at your **Learning Center Schedule** worksheet. First, you need to increase the cell width for the row labels in column A. Here are five ways to accomplish that task. Of course, you only need to do one of them. But do read through all five ways, so that you are familiar with them.

1. Move your cell pointer between the column headings A and B. When the cell pointer is positioned on the line separating the headings, it changes to an adjust arrow. Double click the mouse button when you see the adjust arrow and watch the column width increase automatically to accommodate the text.

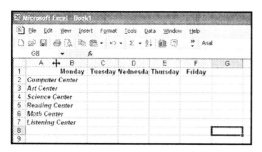 

—or—

2. Move your cell pointer between the column headings A and B. When the cell pointer is positioned on the line separating the headings, it changes to an adjust arrow. Click and drag the adjust arrow to the desired column width.

—or—

3. Click on **column heading A** to select (highlight) the entire column.

4. Then **Format** on the Menu bar.

5. Click **Column**.

6. Click **Width**.

7. At the Column Width window, change the column width from its default setting to **20**.

8. Then click **OK**.

9. Click in any empty cell to remove the highlighting from column A and view the changes you made.

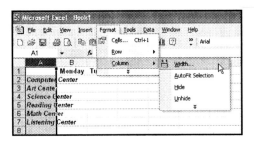 

—or—

10. Click on **column heading A** to select (highlight) the entire column.

11. Then click **Format** on the Menu bar.

12. Click **Column**.

13. Click **AutoFit Selection**. The width will adjust automatically to the widest entry in the column.

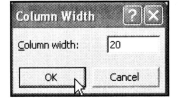 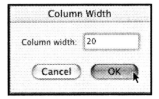

14. Click in any empty cell to remove the highlighting from column A and view the changes you made.

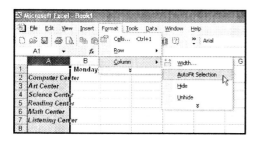 

—or—

15. Click on **column heading A** to select (highlight) the entire column.

16. Click the right mouse button anywhere within column A.

Note: If you are using a Mac, hold down the **Control** key on your keyboard and click on **column A**.

17. Select **Column Width**.

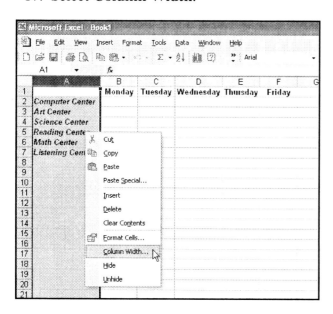 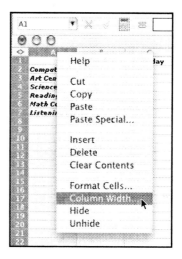

18. At the Column Width window, change the column width from its default setting to **20**.

19. Then click **OK**.

20. Then click in any empty cell to remove the highlighting from column A and view the changes you made.

Now that you have all five techniques fresh in your mind, adjust the width of column D so that this column label has sufficient cell space. If necessary, review the above steps substituting column D for all references to column A.

Note: If you are using a Mac, you do not need to adjust the width of column D. *Microsoft Excel* automatically adjusted the width as you used the AutoFill feature.

Does your worksheet look like this? Great!

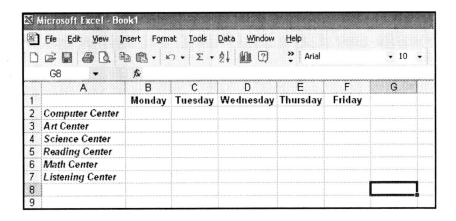

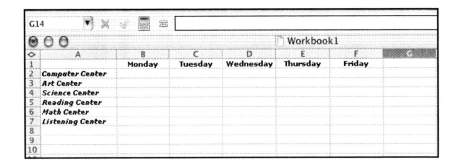

Activity 4—Saving, Using, and Renaming a Workbook Template

Now that you have the learning center schedule set up and ready for entering student names, it is important to save it as a workbook template first. By saving it without student names, the learning center schedule template will always be ready for you to use again and again, week after week, or whenever you decide to change your learning center assignments.

Saving the Learning Center Schedule Template

1. Click on the **File** menu and select **Save** or click the **Save** button on the Standard toolbar.

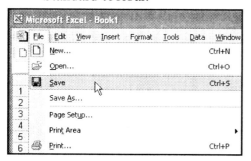 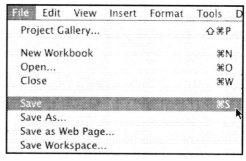

2. At the **Save As** window, click the **Save as type** list arrow (**Format** on the Mac) and select **Template**.

Note: Notice that when you selected Template on the PC, *Microsoft Excel* automatically navigated to a Templates folder. This is where your template file will be stored until the next time that you need it. (You will be shown how to access the template file at the end of this activity.) On the Mac, *Excel* navigates to the **My Templates** folder.

3. In the **File name** textbox (**Name** on the Mac), change the file name from **Book1** (**Workbook1** on the Mac) to **Learning Center Schedule Template**. If you are using a Mac, change the name to **Learning Center Schedule**. You cannot have a file name that exceeds 31 characters on a Mac.

4. Then click **Save**.

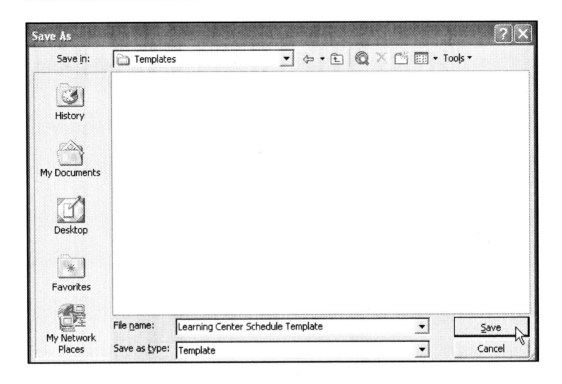

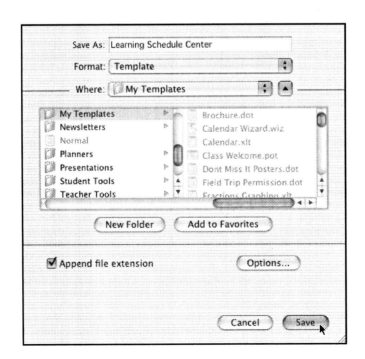

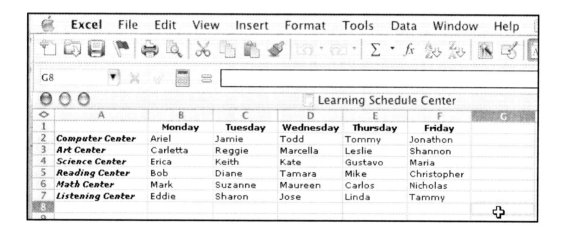

Using the Learning Center Schedule Template

Now that the learning center schedule template is saved, you're ready to use it. So, enter student first names in cells B2 through F6. Pick any student first names you wish. Practice some of your navigation techniques along the way.

If you notice that any of your student first names are wider than the column widths, you know how to adjust for that too!

Renaming the Learning Center Schedule Template

Now that the student first names are entered, it is time to save the learning center schedule again.

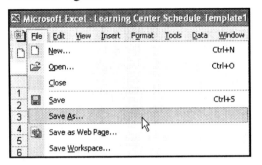 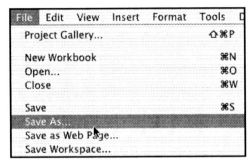

5. Click on the **File** menu and select **Save As**.

6. At the Save As window, change the file name from **Learning Center Schedule Template** to **Learning Center Schedule for January** (for Mac users, due to character limitations, just change it to **Learning Center January**), navigate to where you wish to save your file, and click on **Save**.

7. Now that you have saved, used, and renamed the learning center schedule template, print a copy for your class.

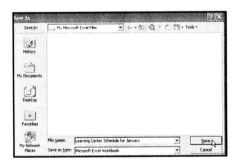 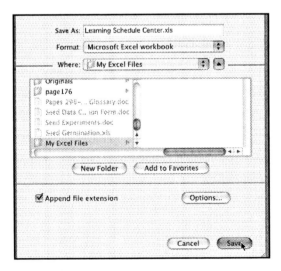

A Special Note about Accessing the Learning Center Schedule Template

Imagine that January is over and you are ready to open your **Learning Center Schedule Template** and create a new schedule for February. How do you access the Template folder where *Microsoft Excel* automatically saved your template file?

When you launch *Microsoft Excel* on the PC, you will see a **New Workbook** task pane on the right-hand side of your screen. (If you don't see a New Workbook task pane, click **View** on the Menu bar and select **Task Pane**. It will appear.) Under **New from template**, click **General Template**. Click the **General** tab to bring it to the forefront, if necessary. You will see your **Learning Center Schedule Template** file listed there. Simply click on the template file to select it. Then click **OK**. The **Learning Center Schedule Template** file appears on your screen, ready for your input.

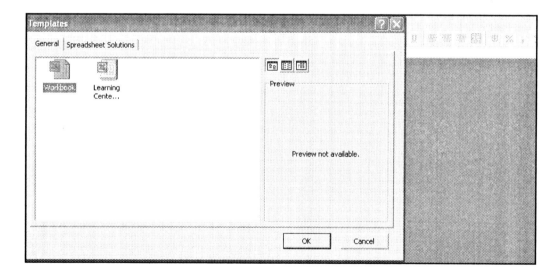

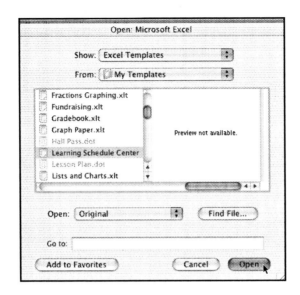

If you are using a Mac, after launching *Microsoft Excel*, click **File** on the Menu bar. Click **Open**. At the Open window, click the **Show** list arrow and select **Excel Templates**. Navigate to the folder where you saved your **Learning Center Schedule Template** file. Click the workbook file to select it. Then click **Open**.

Activity 5—Printing and Closing a Workbook

In this activity you will print your **Learning Center Schedule for January** and learn how to close the workbook file properly before exiting *Microsoft Excel*.

Note: Although your worksheet has 65,536 rows and 256 columns, *Microsoft Excel* only prints the area where you have been working. Pretty smart program, eh?

Printing the Learning Center Schedule

1. To print your **Learning Center Schedule for January**, click **File** on the Menu bar.
2. Click **Print**.

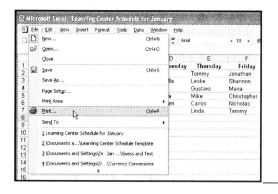   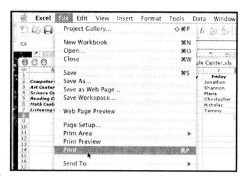

or—

3. Click the **Print** button on the Standard toolbar.

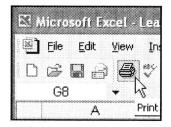   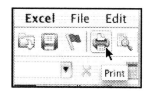

4. If you printed using the File/Print command, a Print window will appear. At the Print window, simply click **OK**.

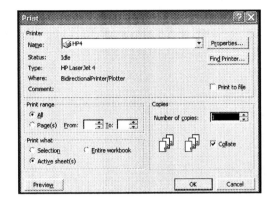 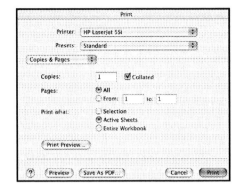

Closing the Learning Center Schedule Workbook

5. To close the **Learning Center Schedule for January**, click **File** on the Menu bar.

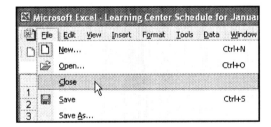 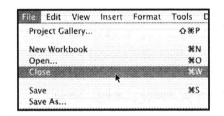

6. Click **Close**.

—or—

7. Click on the **Close Window** button for the workbook.

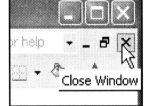 

Exiting *Microsoft Excel*

That's it for the **Learning Center Schedule**! So exit *Microsoft Excel* for now. Get up and stretch. Take a look out the window to rest your eyes. Pick up your **Learning Center Schedule** for January from the printer. Nice job!

Activity 6—Creating Vertical Column Labels

Imagine that as part of the school-wide reading incentive program, your principal announced that she would throw a pizza party for every class that demonstrated a 100 percent increase in student reading over the next six weeks. Your tasks are to find out how many books your students read last week (to use as a baseline) and to keep track of your students' reading for the next six weeks. No sweat! Recording the data you collect in a worksheet will make your job easy!

In this activity you will open a new *Microsoft Excel* workbook and start to develop a reading progress worksheet. In doing so, you'll also have a chance to quickly review how to enter and format column labels. Then comes the real fun! You'll learn how to rotate the standard horizontal column labels, making them vertical. Let's get started!

Getting Started

1. Launch *Microsoft Excel*. If *Microsoft Excel* is already running and a workbook is not displayed on your screen, open a new one. Click **File** on the Menu bar.

2. Then click **New**. (**New Workbook** for a Mac.)

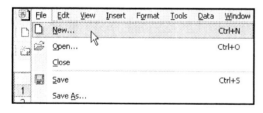 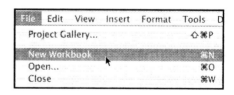

—or—

3. Click the **New** button on the Standard toolbar.

Entering Column Labels Using AutoFill

First you'll enter the weeks you'll be recording reading progress as column labels.

4. Click in cell **B1** and type the column label **Week 0**.

Note: Be sure to use the number zero (0) rather than a capital letter O so that you can use the AutoFill feature.

5. Use the **AutoFill** feature to complete the remaining column labels **Week 1** through **Week 6**.

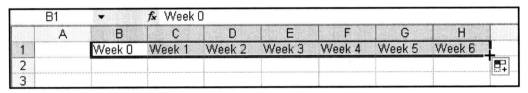

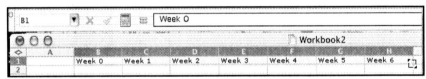

Note: If you don't remember how to use the AutoFill feature, here's a quick review. Using your mouse, point to the fill handle—the small square at the bottom-right corner of the active cell (B1). When the cell pointer is positioned on the fill handle, it changes to a black cross. Click on the black cross and drag the fill handle to the right, highlighting cells C1 through H1. Release the mouse button. Week 1 through Week 6 automatically appear.

Formatting Column Labels

6. Format the column labels (**Week 0** through **Week 6**), making them **Bold** and **Italic**.

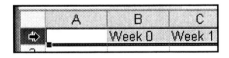

Note: If you don't remember how to format column labels, here's a quick review. Click on **row heading 1**. The entire row highlights, allowing you to apply the following formatting commands to the selected cells. Click the **Bold** button (**B**) on

the Formatting toolbar to bold Week 0 through Week 6. Click on the **Italic** button (**I**) on the Formatting toolbar to italicize Week 0 through Week 6. If you don't see the **Italic** button (**I**) on the Formatting toolbar, don't panic! Simply click the list arrow at the end of the Formatting toolbar. Several more formatting buttons will display. Then find and click on the **Italic** button (**I**).

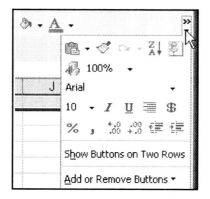

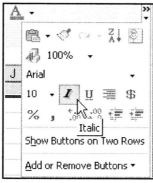

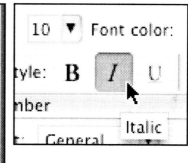

Click on any empty cell in the worksheet to remove the highlighting from row 1 and view the formatting changes made.

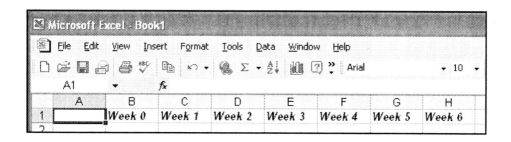

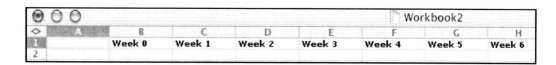

Creating Vertical Column Labels

Ready to change your column labels from a horizontal format to a vertical format? This task is especially helpful if your column labels are much wider than the data you will be entering.

7. Click the row heading 1 to select (highlight) the entire row.

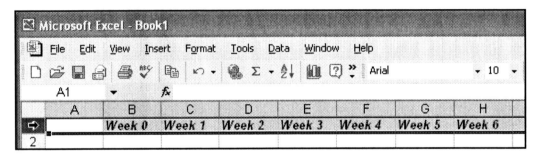

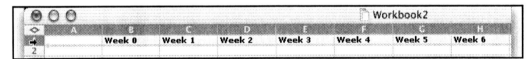

8. Click **Format** on the Menu bar.

9. Click **Cells**.

10. Click the **Alignment** tab to bring it to the forefront.

11. Under Text alignment, click the Horizontal list arrow and select Center.

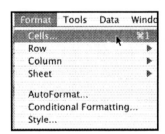

12. Change the Orientation from 0 degrees to **90** degrees. You can do this in one of three ways. First, you can simply highlight the 0 and type **90** in the **Degrees** box. Second, you can click the up arrow next to the 0 until it reaches 90 degrees. Third, you can click and drag the text line upward until it reaches 90 degrees.

As you are dragging the text line upward, watch the numbers change from 0 to 90 in the Degrees box.

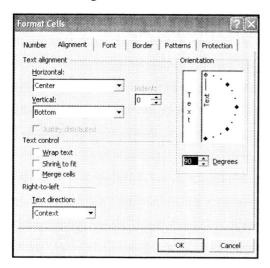 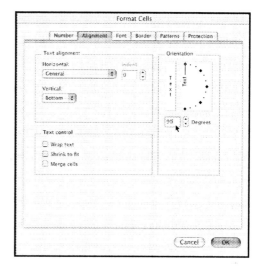

13. When you are finished, click **OK**.

When you return to your worksheet, notice that the column labels are now vertical and centered. Neat! However, the cells are much wider than necessary to record the number of books your students read each week. So, adjust the column width!

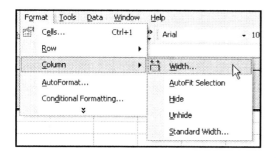 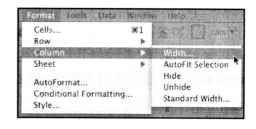

Adjusting Column Widths

14. While row 1 is still highlighted, click **Format** on the Menu bar.
15. Click **Column**.
16. Click **Width**.
17. At the **Column Width** window, change the column width to **5**.
18. Then click **OK**. That should be plenty wide!

Click in any empty cell to remove the highlighting from Week 0 through Week 6 and view the vertical column labels you created and formatted.

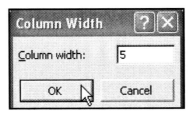

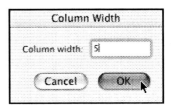

Well done!

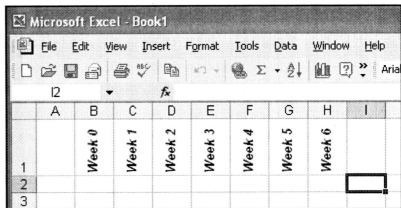

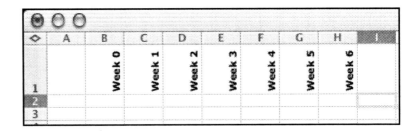

Activity 7—Entering Row Labels Using AutoFill

Now that the column labels are displayed in the reading progress worksheet, you're ready for the next task—entering row labels. Here you have two options. You can either type actual student names in cell A2 through A31 (boring!) or you can use the AutoFill feature to quickly enter fictitious student names. I prefer using the AutoFill, of course. How about you?

Entering Row Labels Using AutoFill

1. Click in cell **A2**, type **Student 1**, and press the Enter or Return key on your keyboard.

2. Since the Student 1 row label is wider than column A, adjust the column width as follows. Move your cell pointer between column headings A and B. When the cell pointer is positioned on the line separating the headings, it changes to an adjust arrow. Double click the mouse button when you see the adjust arrow and watch the column width increase automatically to accommodate the text.

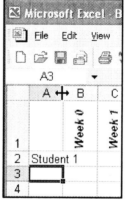

3. Use the AutoFill feature to complete the remaining row labels Student 2 through Student 30.

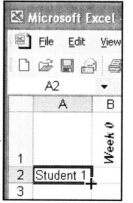

Note: If you don't remember how to use the AutoFill feature, here's a quick review. Using your mouse, point to the fill handle— the small square at the bottom-right corner of the active cell (A2). When the cell pointer is positioned on the fill handle, it changes to a black cross. Click on the black cross and drag the fill handle down, highlighting cells A3 through A31. Release the mouse button. Student 2 through Student 30 automatically appears.

Another Note: Since you are filling all the way down to cell A31, don't panic and let go of the fill handle when you reach the bottom of your screen. Continue dragging downward. The worksheet will scroll down with you.

Didn't get it right? No problem. Just click in any empty cell to remove the highlighting. Then scroll back up, click in cell A2, and try again. Your new AutoFill will replace any text displayed in the cells.

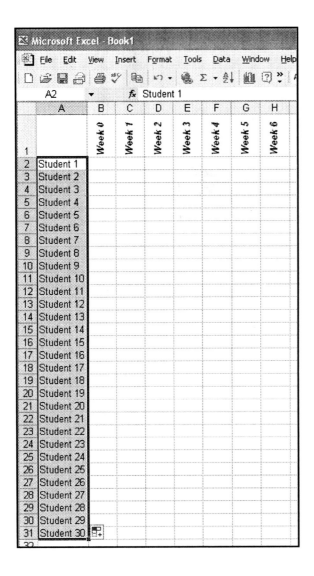

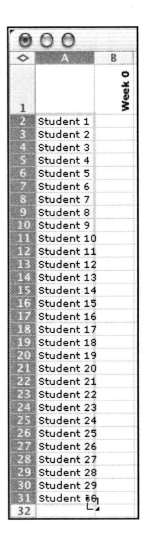

4. Click on any empty cell in the worksheet to remove the highlighting from column A and view the list of students.

5. Notice that several of the row labels (those with two digits) are wider than column A. So, adjust the column width again.

Well, there are some other formatting changes that can be made to the row labels. Ready to play with a little color? Great!

Activity 8—Changing the Text Color

In this activity, you'll continue formatting the row labels. However, you'll add a touch of color to the text. Even if you only have a black and white printer, it's still fun to play with color to enhance the look of your worksheet. When it comes time to print, the colors you select simply print as gray tones.

Formatting the Row Labels

1. To begin, format the row labels (Student 1 through Student 30), making them bold.

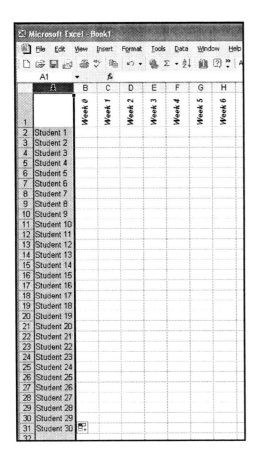
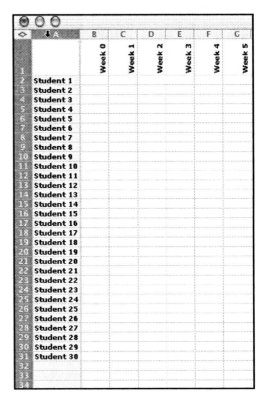

Note: If you don't remember how for format row labels, here's a quick review. Click on the **column heading A** to select (highlight) the entire column. Click the **Bold** button on the Formatting toolbar to bold Student 1 through Student 30.

2. Now to add some color. With column A still selected (highlighted), click on the **Font Color** button on the Formatting toolbar.

3. In the Font Color drop-down window, change the font color from black to blue, red, or any one of your favorite colors displayed.

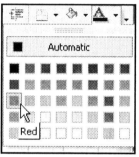
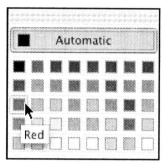

4. Click in any empty cell to remove the highlighting from column A and view the formatting changes you've made.

Now that your reading progress worksheet is ready to enter student reading data, it's a good idea to save it. You wouldn't want to start from scratch, just in case something happened to your computer system, would you? Didn't think so!

Saving the Reading Progress Workbook

5. To save your reading progress worksheet, click **File** on the Menu bar.
6. Click **Save As....**

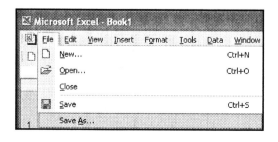
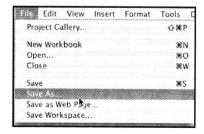

—or—

7. Click the **Save** button on the Standard toolbar.

8. At the **Save As** window, click the Save in list arrow and navigate to the folder where you want to save your workbook file.

9. Click in the **File name** textbox and change the file name from **Book1** to **Reading Progress**.

10. Then click **Save**.

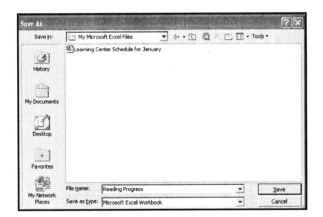 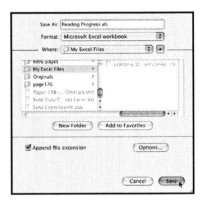

Well, are you ready to start entering student reading data? Don't moan. Since you are using fictitious students, you can also use fictitious figures. So, in the next activity you'll learn how to copy and paste blocks of numbers to save time. Doesn't that sound better?

Activity 9—Selecting, Copying, and Pasting Data

Recording your students' reading progress will actually provide you with an opportunity to practice essential selecting, copying, and pasting skills within a worksheet. In this activity, you'll perform these skills vertically first and horizontally second. Remember that practice makes perfect!

Getting Started

1. Open your **Reading Progress** workbook (used in Activities 6, 7, and 8), if it is not already opened.

Note: To open your Reading Progress workbook, click **File** on the Menu bar. You may see your workbook file listed. If so, simply click on the file to open it.

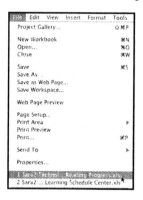

If not, click **Open**. (You can also click the **Open** button on the Standard toolbar.)

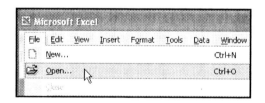
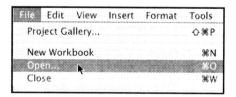

At the **Open** window, navigate to where you saved the workbook. Then double-click on the **Reading Progress** workbook file to select and open it.

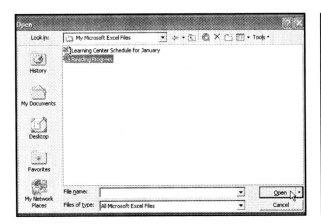 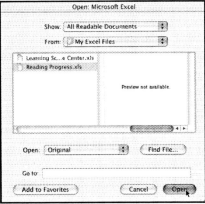

Entering Data

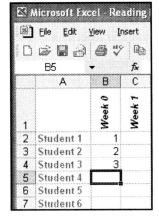

2. Click in cell **B2** and type **1**, indicating that Student 1 read one book last week.

3. Click in cell **B3** and type **2**, indicating the Student 2 read two books last week.

4. Click in cell **B4** and type **3**, indicating the Student 3 read three books last week.

You discover that Student 4, Student 5, and Student 6 read 1, 2, and 3 books, respectively, as well. So, rather than typing in the numbers, you can simply select, copy, and paste cells B2 though B4 into cells B5 through B7.

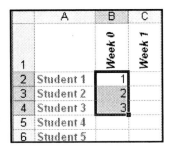 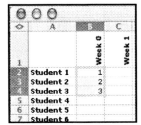

Selecting Data Vertically

5. Select (highlight) cells **B2 through B4**. The numbers 1 through 3 should be highlighted.

Copying Data

6. Click **Edit** on the Menu bar.

7. Click **Copy**.

—or—

8. Click the **Copy** button on the Standard toolbar.

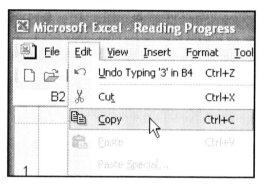 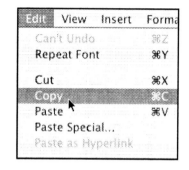

Note: Notice that there are "marching ants" around cells **B2 through B4**. *Microsoft Excel* has copied these cells and is now waiting for your instructions as to where to paste them.

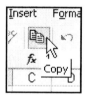

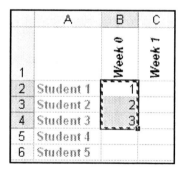 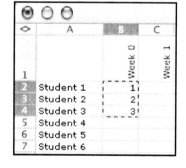

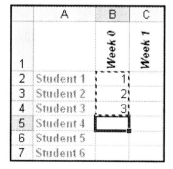 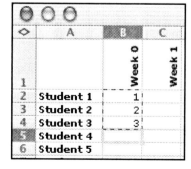

Pasting Data Vertically

9. Click in cell **B5** (which corresponds to Student 4).

10. Click **Edit** on the Menu bar.

11. Click **Paste**.

—or—

12. Click the **Paste** button on the Standard toolbar.

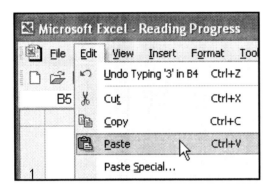 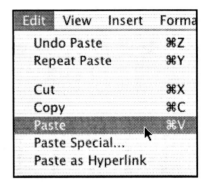

Note: The numbers 1, 2, and 3 should appear in cells B5, B6, and B7 (which correspond to Student 4, Student 5, and Student 6).

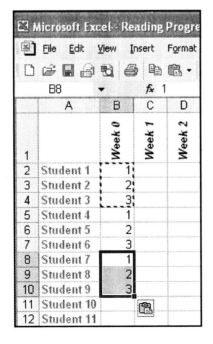 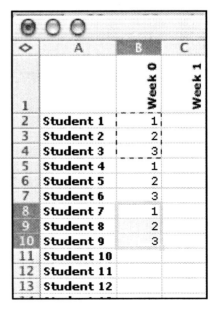

13. Click in cell **B8** and paste again.

Note: The numbers 1, 2, and 3 should appear in cells B8, B9, and B10 (which correspond to Student 7, Student 8, and Student 9).

Now you have recorded baseline reading data for Student 1 through Student 9.

14. Click in cell **B11** and type the following: **4**

Note: Notice that the "marching ants" have now disappeared from around cells B2 though B4 since *Microsoft Excel* detects that you are finished copying and pasting.

	A	B (Week 0)	C (Week 1)
1			
2	Student 1	1	
3	Student 2	2	
4	Student 3	3	
5	Student 4	1	
6	Student 5	2	
7	Student 6	3	
8	Student 7	1	
9	Student 8	2	
10	Student 9	3	
11	Student 10	4	
12	Student 11		

	A	B (Week 0)	C (Week 1)
1			
2	Student 1	1	
3	Student 2	2	
4	Student 3	3	
5	Student 4	1	
6	Student 5	2	
7	Student 6	3	
8	Student 7	1	
9	Student 8	2	
10	Student 9	3	
11	Student 10	4	
12	Student 11		

So, did you get the "knack" of selecting, copying, and pasting? It's not too hard. And it can save you a lot of time.

Next, try selecting, copying, and pasting horizontally. It's just as easy. We just want to make sure you feel comfortable working in both directions. Ready?

Entering Data
15. Click in cell **C2** and type the following: **2**
16. Click in cell **D2** and type the following: **3**
17. Click in cell **E2** and type the following: **4**

Selecting Data Horizontally

18. Select (highlight) cells **C2 through E2**.

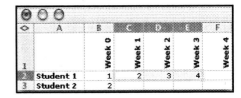

Copying Data

19. Click **Edit** on the Menu bar.

20. Click **Copy**.

—or—

21. Click the **Copy** button on the Standard toolbar.

Note: Notice that there are "marching ants" around cells C2 through E2. *Microsoft Excel* has copied these cells and is now waiting for your instructions as to where to paste them.

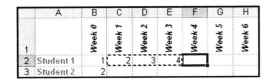
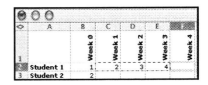

Pasting Data Horizontally

22. Click in cell **F2** (which corresponds to Week 3).

23. Click **Edit** on the Menu bar.

24. Click **Paste**.

—or—

25. Click the **Paste** button on the Standard toolbar.

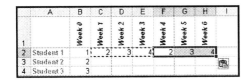

Note: The numbers 2, 3, and 4 should appear in cells F2, G2, and H2 (which correspond to Week 4, Week 5, and Week 6).

Now you have recorded data for Student 1's reading progress.

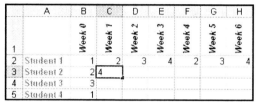 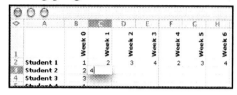

26. Click in cell **C3** and type the following: 4

Note: Notice that the "marching ants" have now disappeared from around cells F2 though H2 since *Microsoft Excel* detects that you are finished copying and pasting.

Saving the Reading Progress Workbook

Just so you don't lose the changes you've made to your reading progress worksheet, save it.

27. Click **File** on the Menu bar.
28. Click **Save**.

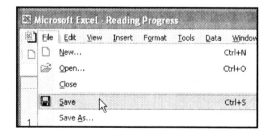 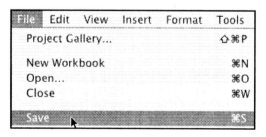

—or—

29. Click the Save button
    on the Standard toolbar.

Note: The Save As window will not
appear this time, since you already
saved this file before. The program
assumes that unless you select File/Save As, you want the file saved under the
same name and in the same place as you already saved it.

Fill down and fill right are two more *Microsoft Excel* features that can save you
time. You'll learn how to use them to enter data in the next activity.

Activity 10—Using the Fill-Down and Fill-Right Features

You've already seen how selecting, copying, and pasting can save you time. The fill-down and fill-right features speed up your data entry work as well. They are useful if you have values that are repeated. Rather than typing the values again and again, you can simply select them and use the fill-down or fill-right feature to enter the values quickly. Here's your chance to try both fill-down and fill-right features.

Getting Started

1. Open your **Reading Progress** workbook (used in Activities 6, 7, 8, and 9), if it is not already opened.

Note: To open your **Reading Progress** workbook, click **File** on the Menu bar. You may see your workbook file listed. If so, simply click on the file to open it.

If not, click **Open**. (You can also click the **Open** button on the Standard toolbar.) At the **Open** window, navigate to where you saved the workbook. Then double-click on the **Reading Progress** workbook file to select and open it.

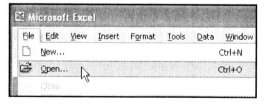 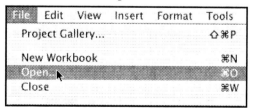

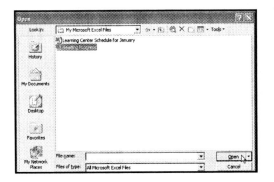

Using the Fill-Down Feature

You suddenly realize that the next seven students have all read four books. Rather than typing in the numbers, you can use the fill-down feature so that *Microsoft Excel enters* the data for you.

When you use the fill-down feature, you must begin in the cell that has the data you wish to replicate. In this case, Student 10 has read 4 books. Therefore, you can use the data in cell B11 as the starting point for your fill.

2. Click in cell **B11** and drag down to cell **B18**, selecting (highlighting) cells B11 through B18.

Note: In this instance, you are **not** using the fill handle, as you have learned to do using the AutoFill feature. Rather, you are merely highlighting from cell B11 through cell B18.

If you reach the bottom of your screen before reaching cell B18, keep dragging. The worksheet will scroll with you. Cells B11 through B18 should be highlighted.

Didn't get it right? No problem. Just click in any empty cell to remove the highlighting. Then scroll back up, if necessary, click in cell B11, and try again.

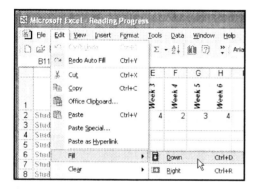 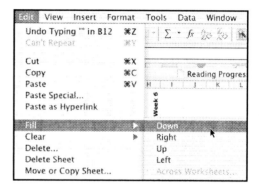

3. With cells B11 through B18 selected, click **Edit** on the Menu bar.
4. Click **Fill**.
5. Click **Down**.

Note: If you don't see the **Fill** option, wait just three seconds. It will appear when the Edit menu expands to display all options.

Notice that cells B11 through B18 now all display the number 4. Click in any empty cell to remove the highlighting from cells B11 through B18 and view the fill you completed.

Using the Fill-Right Feature

You realize that Student 2 read four books consistently from Week 1 through Week 6. You already have the number of books read (4) recorded for Week 1. You can use the fill-right feature to complete your data entry quickly.

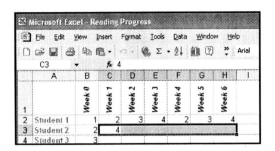 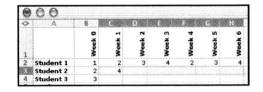

6. Click in cell **C3** and drag through cell **H3** selecting (highlighting) cells C3 through H3.

Note: Remember that when you use the fill-right feature, you must begin in the cell that has the data you wish to replicate.

7. With cells C3 though H3 selected, click on **Edit** on the Menu bar.
8. Click **Fill**.
9. Click **Right**.

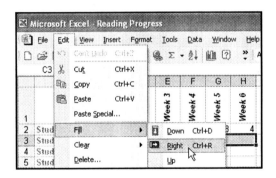 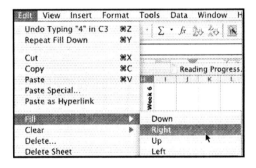

Note: Notice that cells C3 though H3 now all display the number 4.

Click in any empty cell to remove the highlighting from cells C3 through H3 and view the fill you completed.

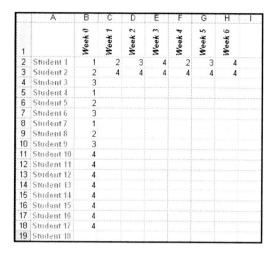
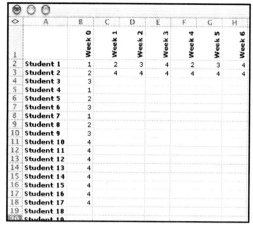

Feel free to practice using the fill-down and fill-right features on your own. You can also practice selecting, copying, and pasting a few more times, as you will not be using this worksheet for the next activity.

Saving the Workbook

After you're done practicing your fill-down, fill-right, selecting, copying, and pasting skills, save the Reading Progress workbook.

10. Click **File** on the Menu bar.

11. Click **Save**.

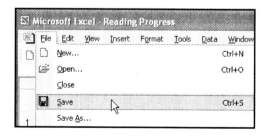
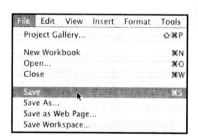

—or—

12. Click the **Save** button on the Standard toolbar.

Note: The Save As window will not appear this time, since you already saved this file before. The program assumes that unless you select File/Save As, you want the file saved under the same name and in the same place as you already saved it.

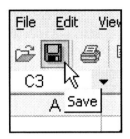

Closing the Workbook

Since you will not be using this workbook for your next activity, close it.

13. Click **File** on the Menu bar.

14. Click **Close**.

—or—

15. Click the **Close Window** button for the workbook.

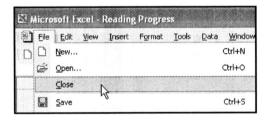

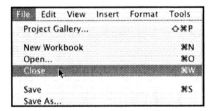

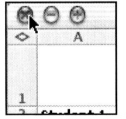

Exiting Excel

That's it for the **Reading Progress** worksheet. So exit *Excel* for now. Get up and stretch. Take a look out the window to rest your eyes. You'll continue with a new **Reading Progress Data** worksheet in the next activity—one that already has all the data entered for you.

Activity 11—Setting Horizontal and Vertical Split Lines

In this activity you'll learn how to split your worksheet into several panes to help keep you oriented. This skill is especially helpful when you work with really large worksheets.

Getting Started

1. Open the **Reading Progress Data** workbook that is on the CD. (You will find the CD in the back of this *Microsoft Excel for Terrified Teachers* book.)

Note: To open the **Reading Progress Data** workbook, place the CD in the CD drive of your computer system. Launch *Microsoft Excel*, if it is not already running. Click **File** on the Menu bar. Click **Open**.

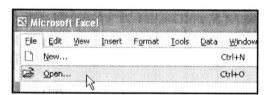 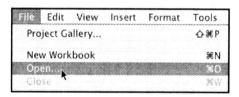

(You can also click the **Open** button on the Standard toolbar.) At the Open window, navigate to the CD drive. Then click on the **Reading Progress Data** workbook to select it. Click **Open**.

You will find that the data for the student **Reading Progress Data** workbook has already been entered for you in order to save time.

2. Scroll down to row **32**.

Notice that as you scroll down, you lose sight of the column headings (A, B, C, etc.) and the column labels (Week 0 through Week 6). Of course, this is a small worksheet covering only 248 cells. You can probably remember the column labels and can figure out where you are without seeing them. But imagine how it would be if you had a huge worksheet with several more column labels. It would be easy to become disoriented once the column headings and column labels disappeared. You would have to keep scrolling up and down to make sure you were entering data into the correct columns.

Likewise, in a very wide worksheet, you could lose sight of the row headings (1, 2, 3, etc.) and the row labels (Student 1 through Student 30). Then you would have to keep scrolling left and right to make sure you were entering data into the correct rows.

What a bother all that scrolling would be! In fact, you probably wouldn't want to use a worksheet if entering data was that cumbersome.

Thankfully, *Microsoft Excel* has designed the worksheet so it can be split into four panes— three of which are scrollable. You can set one of the panes to show your column headings and column labels at all times. You can set one of the panes to show your row headings and row labels at all times. Then can use the third pane to move around your worksheet, entering data. You will never become disoriented because the column headings, column labels, row headings, and row labels for the area you are working on will always be in view.

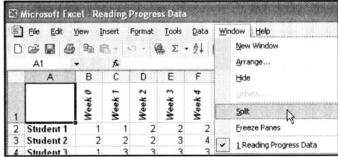

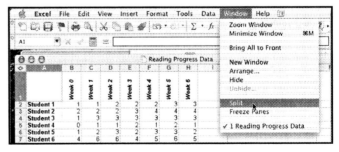

So, you need to know how to split the worksheet into panes and set the horizontal and vertical split lines. Here goes!

Splitting the Worksheet

3. Scroll back up and click in cell **A1**, making it your active cell.
4. Click **Window** on the Menu bar.
5. Click Split.

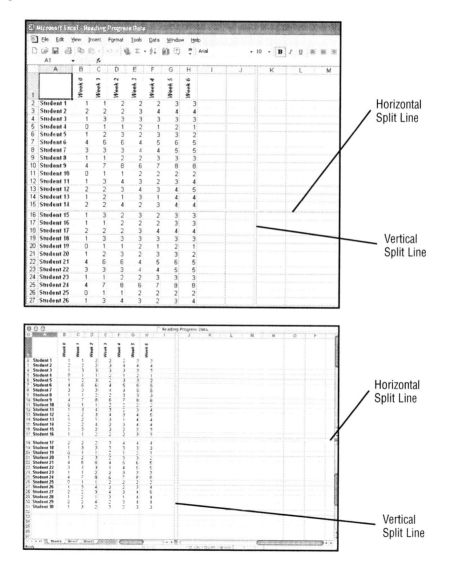

Note: If you don't see the **Split** option, just wait three seconds. It will appear when the Window menu expands to display all options.

Notice that a vertical split line and a horizontal split line appear on your worksheet. Can you see that your worksheet has been split into four panes? Good.

Three out of four of the panes have scrollbars. Since the upper-left pane has no scroll bar, it's not scrollable. You won't be working with that pane at all.

The upper-right pane has a vertical scrollbar. The lower-left pane has a horizontal scrollbar. And the lower-right pane has both a horizontal scrollbar and a vertical scrollbar.

The first thing you do when you split your worksheet is set the horizontal and vertical split lines. You are going to set the split lines so that the column headings, column labels, row headings, and row labels will always show. Here's how.

6. Move your cursor over the horizontal split line. When the cursor changes to a move arrow, click and drag the horizontal split line up until it is on the separating line between rows 1 and 2—right under your column headings and column labels. Release the mouse button.

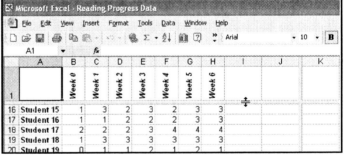

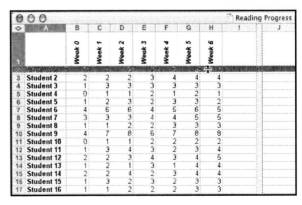

Note: If you released your mouse button before the horizontal split line was perfectly in place, just try again. If you moved the horizontal split line too far up and it

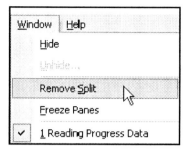

far up and it disappeared, start over. Click **Window** on the Menu bar and select **Remove Split** to clear the worksheet. Then click **Window** on the Menu bar again. Select **Split**. Try again.

7. Once the horizontal split line is in place under the column headings and column labels, move your cursor over the vertical split line. When the cursor changes to a move arrow, click and drag the vertical split line to the left until it is on the separating line between columns A and B—

immediately to the right of the row headings and row labels. Release the mouse button.

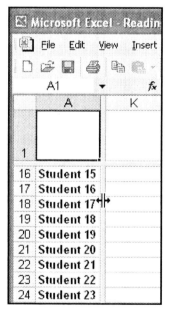

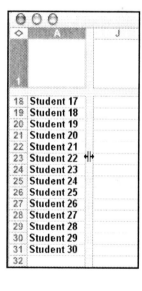

Note: If you released your mouse button before the vertical split line was perfectly in place, just try again. If you moved the vertical split line too far to the left and it disappeared, start over. Click **Window** on the Menu bar and select **Remove Split** to clear the worksheet. Then click

Window on the Menu bar again. Select **Split**. Try again. Of course, you'll have to reset the horizontal split line as well.

Note: Don't panic if most of your data seems to disappear. You'll scroll to get it back.

8. Using the horizontal scroll bar in the lower-right pane, scroll to the left until your columns are back in A, B, C order and you can see Week 0 through Week 6 in the upper-right pane.

Note: If you scroll too far to the left and the row labels (Student 1 through Student 30) are displayed twice (in the lower-left pane and in the lower-right pane), scroll back to the right until the row labels in the lower-right pane are out of sight.

9. Using the vertical scroll bar in the lower-right pane, scroll up until your rows are in 1, 2, 3 order and you can see Student 1, Student 2, Student 3, etc., in the lower-left pane.

Note: If you scroll too far up and the column labels are displayed twice (in the upper-right pane and the lower-right pane), scroll back down until the column labels in the lower-right pane are out of sight and you regain 1, 2, 3 order.

	A	B Week 0	C Week 1	D Week 2	E Week 3	F Week 4	G Week 5	H Week 6	I
1									
2	Student 1	1	1	2	2	2	3	3	
3	Student 2	2	2	2	3	4	4	4	
4	Student 3	1	3	3	3	3	3	3	
5	Student 4	0	1	1	2	1	2	1	
6	Student 5	1	2	3	2	3	3	2	
7	Student 6	4	6	6	4	5	6	5	
8	Student 7	3	3	3	4	4	5	5	
9	Student 8	1	1	2	2	3	3	3	
10	Student 9	4	7	8	6	7	8	8	
11	Student 10	0	1	1	2	2	2	2	
12	Student 11	1	3	4	3	2	3	4	
13	Student 12	2	2	3	4	3	4	5	
14	Student 13	1	2	1	3	1	4	4	
15	Student 14	2	2	4	2	3	4	4	
16	Student 15	1	3	2	3	2	3	3	
17	Student 16	1	1	2	2	2	3	3	
18	Student 17	2	2	2	3	4	4	4	
19	Student 18	1	3	3	3	3	3	3	
20	Student 19	0	1	1	2	1	2	1	
21	Student 20	1	2	3	2	3	3	2	
22	Student 21	4	6	6	4	5	6	5	

	Week 0	Week 1	Week 2	Week 3	Week 4	Week 5	Week 6
Student 1	1	1	2	2	2	3	3
Student 2	2	2	2	3	4	4	4
Student 3	1	3	3	3	3	3	3
Student 4	0	1	1	2	1	2	1
Student 5	1	2	3	2	3	3	2
Student 6	4	6	6	4	5	6	5
Student 7	3	3	3	4	4	5	5
Student 8	1	1	2	2	3	3	3
Student 9	4	7	8	6	7	8	8
Student 10	0	1	1	2	2	2	2
Student 11	1	3	4	3	2	3	4
Student 12	2	2	3	4	3	4	5
Student 13	1	2	1	3	1	4	4
Student 14	2	2	4	2	3	4	4
Student 15	1	3	2	3	2	3	3
Student 16	1	1	2	2	2	3	3
Student 17	2	2	2	3	4	4	4
Student 18	1	3	3	3	3	3	3
Student 19	0	1	1	2	1	2	1
Student 20	1	2	3	2	3	3	2
Student 21	4	6	6	4	5	6	5
Student 22	3	3	3	4	4	5	5
Student 23	1	1	2	2	3	3	3
Student 24	4	7	8	6	7	8	8
Student 25	0	1	1	2	2	2	2
Student 26	1	3	4	3	2	3	4
Student 27	2	2	3	4	3	4	5
Student 28	1	2	1	3	1	4	4
Student 29	2	2	4	2	3	4	4
Student 30	1	3	2	3	2	3	3

When you are finished scrolling, your worksheet should look like the worksheet displayed on this page. The column headings are in A, B, C order, even with the vertical split line. The row headings are in 1, 2, 3, order, even with the horizontal split line.

Now that your worksheet vertical and horizontal split lines are set properly, you can use the lower-right pane's vertical and horizontal scroll arrows, bars, and lines without ever losing the column labels and row labels associated the area you are working on.

That's it for this activity! In the next activity, you'll be glad your horizontal and vertical split lines are set as you total the students' number of books read.

Activity 12—Using the AutoSum Feature

Of all the great features *Microsoft Excel* has to offer its users, **AutoSum** tops the list. **AutoSum** automatically identifies and adds ranges of cells in your worksheet.

Getting Started

For this activity, your **Reading Progress Data** worksheet should be open and split. If it's not, please go back to **Activity 11** and follow the instructions for opening and splitting the worksheet into four panes. Then return to this activity to learn how to use the AutoSum feature.

	A	B	C	D	E	F	G	H
		Week 0	Week 1	Week 2	Week 3	Week 4	Week 5	Week 6
1								
18	Student 17	2	2	2	3	4	4	4
19	Student 18	1	3	3	3	3	3	3
20	Student 19	0	1	1	2	1	2	1
21	Student 20	1	2	3	2	3	3	2
22	Student 21	4	6	6	4	5	6	5
23	Student 22	3	3	3	4	4	5	5
24	Student 23	1	1	2	2	3	3	3
25	Student 24	4	7	8	6	7	8	8
26	Student 25	0	1	1	2	2	2	2
27	Student 26	1	3	4	3	2	3	4
28	Student 27	2	2	3	4	3	4	5
29	Student 28	1	2	1	3	1	4	4
30	Student 29	2	2	4	2	3	4	4
31	Student 30	1	3	2	3	2	3	3
32	Total							
33								

1. Using the lower-right pane, scroll down the **Reading Progress Data** worksheet until row 32 is displayed.

2. Click in cell **A32** in the lower-left pane and type the following: **Total**

3. Click in cell **B32** in the lower-right pane, making it the active cell. This is where the total number of books read during Week 0 (the baseline week) will be recorded using **AutoSum**.

	A	B	C	D	E	F	G	H
		Week 0	Week 1	Week 2	Week 3	Week 4	Week 5	Week 6
1								
2	Student 1	1	1	2	2	2	3	3
3	Student 2	2	2	2	3	4	4	4
4	Student 3	1	3	3	3	3	3	3
5	Student 4	0	1	1	2	1	2	1
6	Student 5	1	2	3	2	3	3	2
7	Student 6	4	6	6	4	5	6	5
8	Student 7	3	3	3	4	4	5	5
9	Student 8	1	1	2	2	3	3	3
10	Student 9	4	7	8	6	7	8	8
11	Student 10	0	1	1	2	2	2	2
12	Student 11	1	3	4	3	2	3	4
13	Student 12	2	2	3	4	3	4	5
14	Student 13	1	2	1	3	1	4	4
15	Student 14	2	2	4	2	3	4	4
16	Student 15	1	3	2	3	2	3	3
17	Student 16	1	1	2	2	2	3	3
18	Student 17	2	2	2	3	4	4	4
19	Student 18	1	3	3	3	3	3	3
20	Student 19	0	1	1	2	1	2	1
21	Student 20	1	2	3	2	3	3	2
22	Student 21	4	6	6	4	5	6	5
23	Student 22	3	3	3	4	4	5	5
24	Student 23	1	1	2	2	3	3	3
25	Student 24	4	7	8	6	7	8	8
26	Student 25	0	1	1	2	2	2	2
27	Student 26	1	3	4	3	2	3	4
28	Student 27	2	2	3	4	3	4	5
29	Student 28	1	2	1	3	1	4	4
30	Student 29	2	2	4	2	3	4	4
31	Student 30	1	3	2	3	2	3	3
32	Total							

Using AutoSum

We bet you don't want to add up all the numbers in column B in your head or even with a calculator. Fortunately, *Excel* doesn't want you to either. So, it provides you with the AutoSum feature. When you activate AutoSum, it scans your worksheet to determine what cells it "thinks" you want to add up. AutoSum then highlights those cells and places a proposed formula in the active cell. Pretty smart feature, eh?

4. With cell **B32** the active cell, click on the **AutoSum** button (Σ) on the Standard toolbar.

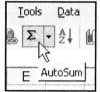
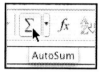

Several things have happened on your worksheet. There are those "marching ants" again! If you scroll up using the vertical scrollbar of the lower-right pane, you'll find that AutoSum has determined that you want to add up all the reading numbers for Week 0 and has selected the appropriate cells (B2 through B31). See how smart AutoSum can be?

AutoSum has also placed the formula for adding up the reading numbers in column B in both cell B32 and the formula bar above the worksheet. Let's "dissect" the formula, so you understand how it works.

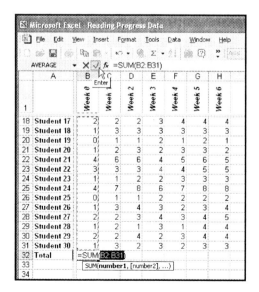
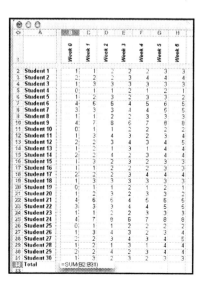

First, there's an equal sign (=). Every formula in *Microsoft Excel* begins with an equal sign. That's how *Microsoft Excel* knows it is a formula rather than just numbers or text.

Second, there's the operation—SUM. You do want to add the reading numbers, right? So, SUM is the appropriate operation.

Third, in the parentheses, there are two cell names or addresses separated by a colon. The two cell addresses are the first cell you want to add and the last cell you want to add. The colon indicates a range. So, rather than having to list every cell you want to add up (B2 + B3 + B4 + B5 + B6 and so on), which would be an awful task, the colon indicates that *Excel* should add up the numbers in all the cells that range from cell B2 through cell B31.

But AutoSum is also very humble. Although admittedly quite "smart," it "knows" it is not infallible. So, AutoSum highlights the range of cells it thinks you want to add up. See the highlighted range in the formula in the active cell? The highlighting allows you to quickly select and substitute another range without having to delete the incorrect display.

5. To indicate that AutoSum has selected the correct range and displayed the correct formula, click the **Enter** button. It is the green check box, to the left of the formula bar.

Once the formula is accepted, the sum appears in the active cell (B32), while the formula still appears in the formula bar—just in case you need to check the formula or make changes.

Well, what do you think about AutoSum so far? Thought you'd like it!

Activity 13—Using AutoFill to Extend Formulas

In this activity you will use the AutoFill feature to extend the formula you created using AutoSum. Although this may sound confusing right now, it's very simple. Let's get clicking!

Getting Started

Your **Reading Progress Data** worksheet should be open, be split (from your completion of **Activity 11**), and display a total value of 48 in cell B32 (from your completion of **Activity 12**).

Now, you could click in cell C32 and activate the AutoSum feature again. Then do the same in cells D32, E32, and so on. However, there's an easier way. You can use AutoFill to extend the formula used in cell C32 to cells D32 through H32 in a single click . . . and drag.

1. Click in cell **B32**, making it the active cell. Use the AutoFill feature to quickly provide the total number of books read for Week 1 though Week 6.

Note: If you don't remember how to use the AutoFill feature, here's a quick review. Using your mouse, point to the fill handle—the small square at the bottom-right corner of the active cell (B32). When the cell pointer is positioned on the fill handle, it changes to a black cross. Click on the black cross and drag it to the right, highlighting cells **C32 through H32**. Release the mouse button. The total number of books read each week automatically appears.

2. Click in any empty cell to remove the highlighting from cells B32 though H32 and view the totals. Bet you never added that fast before!

Before moving on, take a look at what happened when AutoFill extended the formula from cell B32 to the other cells in the row.

3. Click in cell **B32** and look at the formula in the formula bar =SUM(B2:B31).

4. Now click in cell **C32** and look at the formula in the formula bar =SUM(C2:C31). Notice that AutoFill "knew" to adjust the formula in cell B32 relative to what should be added in column C. In other words, AutoFill changed the range from B2:B31 to C2:C31.

The changes that AutoFill made as it copied the formula from one cell to the next are called relative cell references. You'll learn more about relative cell references in upcoming activities.

5. Now click in cells **D32**, **E32**, **F32**, **G32**, and **H32** while watching the formula in the formula bar. Look how AutoFill adjusted the cell ranges in each formula relative to its column.

Well, did your students do it? Did they double the number of books read over the last six weeks? From 48 books read during Week 0 to 112 books read during Week 6, it looks like a pizza party's coming your way! In fact, your students doubled the number of books read during Week 5. Congratulations!

29	Student 28	1	2	1	3	1	4	4
30	Student 29	2	2	4	2	3	4	4
31	Student 30	1	3	2	3	2	3	3
32	Total	48	78	90	90	90	114	112
33								

29	Student 28	1	2	1	3	1	4	4
30	Student 29	2	2	4	2	3	4	4
31	Student 30	1	3	2	3	2	3	3
32	Total	48	78	90	90	90	114	112
33								

6. Before removing the horizontal and vertical split lines from your worksheet, bold the **Total** row to make it more noticeable.

Note: If you don't remember how to bold the **Total** row, here's a quick review. Click the row heading 32 to select (highlight) the entire row. Click the **Bold** button on the Formatting toolbar twice.

Removing the Horizontal and Vertical Splits

Now that you are done with the worksheet, remove the splits.

7. Click **Window** on the Menu bar.
8. Click **Remove Split**.

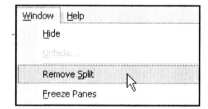 

Voila! The horizontal and vertical split lines are gone!

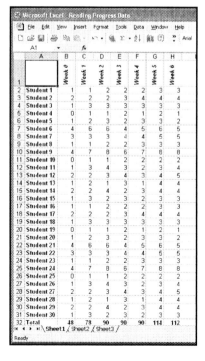 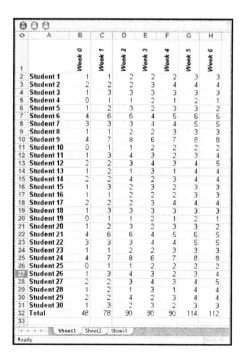

Renaming the Worksheet

Save the **Reading Progress Data** file to your computer system. As you do, rename it.

9. Click **File** on the Menu bar.
10. Click **Save As**.

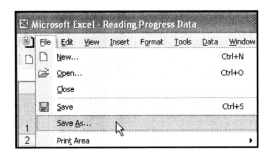 

11. At the **Save As** window, click the **Save in** list arrow and navigate to the folder where you want to save your file.
12. Click in the **File name** textbox and change the file name from Reading **Progress Data** to **Reading Progress Data with Totals**. (If you are using a Mac, just change it to **Reading Progress Totals**.)

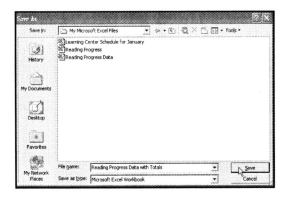 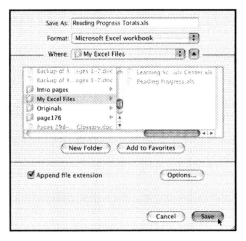

13. Click **Save**.

Closing the Worksheet and Exiting Excel

If you don't have time to go on to the next activity, close the **Reading Progress with Totals** worksheet and exit *Microsoft Excel.* If you do have time, skip the next steps and turn to the next activity.

14. Click **File** on the Menu bar.
15. Click **Close**.

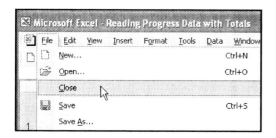
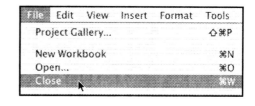

—or—

16. Click the **Close Window** button for the workbook.
17. Then exit *Microsoft Excel.*

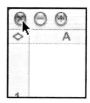

Activity 14—Previewing and Improving the Worksheet

In this activity you'll preview your worksheet to determine what improvements can be made prior to printing. Then you'll add gridlines, insert a title row, merge cells for an expanded title, change the font size, and more. Ready?

Getting Started

1. Open the **Reading Progress Data with Totals** workbook that you worked on in Activity 13, if it is not already open.

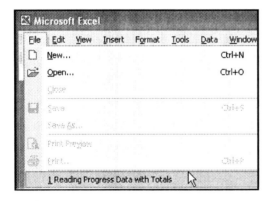
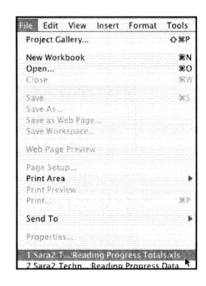

Note: To open your **Reading Progress Data with Totals** workbook, click **File** on the Menu bar. You may see your workbook file listed. If so, simply click on the file to open it. If not, click **Open**. (You can also click the **Open** button on the Standard toolbar.) At the **Open** window, click the **Look in** list arrow and navigate to where you saved the workbook. Then click the **Reading Progress Data with Totals** workbook file to select it. Click **Open**.

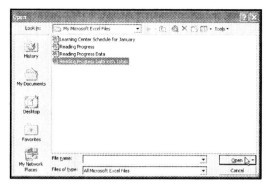

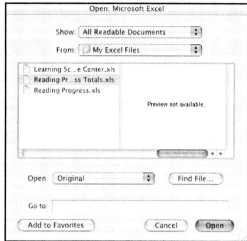

Previewing the Worksheet

2. To preview your worksheet, click **File** on the Menu bar.

3. Click **Print Preview**.

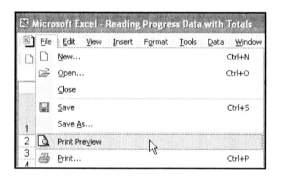

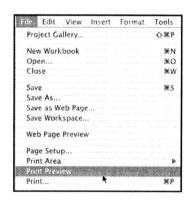

—or—

4. Click the **Print Preview** button on the Standard toolbar.

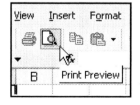

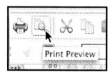

Take a careful look at the previewed worksheet. There are several things you can do before printing the worksheet to make it look better.

First, it looks like the worksheet will print without gridlines. Gridlines are simple to add and tremendously helpful to anyone trying to read your data.

Second, adding a meaningful title would be nice. (Of course, you'll have to insert a row at the top and merge the cells to span the width of the data. That's easy.)

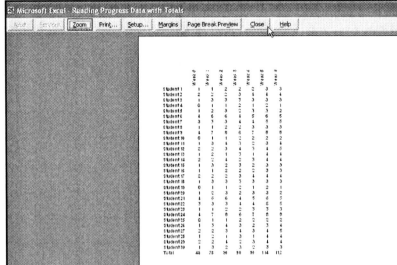

Third, it looks like the font size could be increased, making it easier for the reader.

Ready to tackle all this formatting?

5. Click on the **Close** button to leave the Print Preview and return to the normal worksheet view.

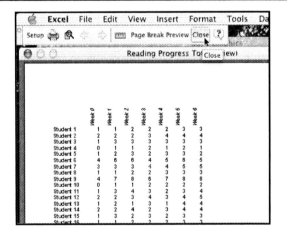

Selecting the Entire Worksheet

6. To select the entire worksheet, click in the blank shaded heading cell in the upper-left corner of the worksheet that is formed by the intersection of the row headings and the column headings. This command selects (highlights) the entire worksheet.

Click Here

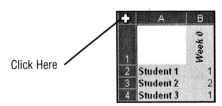

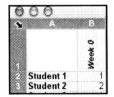

Note: Do not select cell A1. If you selected cell A1 by mistake, the entire worksheet will not highlight. Look just above and to the left of cell A1 where there is a blank heading cell. That's the one! Click there instead.

Adding Gridlines to the Worksheet

7. Click the **Borders** list arrow on the Formatting toolbar.

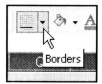 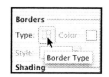

8. Click the **All Borders** option.
9. Click in any blank cell to remove the highlighting from the worksheet and view the gridlines that you have added.

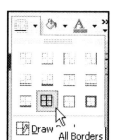 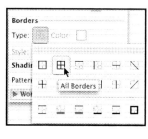

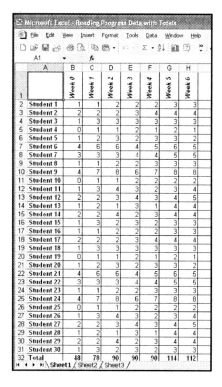 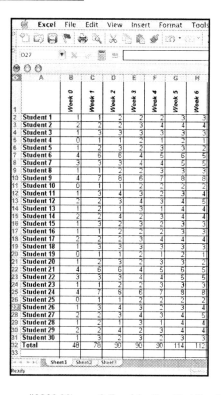

Now that the gridlines are done, get ready to insert a row so that you can add a title to the worksheet. Here goes!

Inserting a Row for the Title

Since the title for the worksheet should be centered above the column labels, you need to insert a row above the first row.

10. Click in cell **A1** to make it the active cell.
11. Click **Insert** on the Menu bar.
12. Click **Rows**.

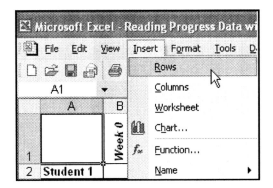 

A new row appears right above the column labels Week 0 through Week 6.

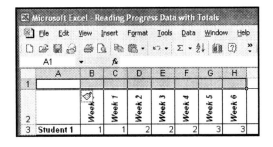 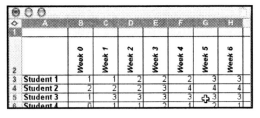

Merging the Cells for the Title

Since you want your title to be centered above the data, you'll have to merge cells A1 through H1, making them one great big cell.

13. Select (highlight) cells **A1 through H1**.

14. Click the **Merge and Center** button on the formatting toolbar.

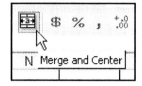

15. In the newly expanded cell **A1** and type the following:
Number of Books Read

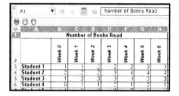

Resizing the Worksheet Font

Your next task is to resize the workbook font, making it larger.

16. Click in the blank shaded heading cell in the upper-left corner of the worksheet that is formed by the intersection of the row headings and the column headings. This command selects (highlights) the entire worksheet.

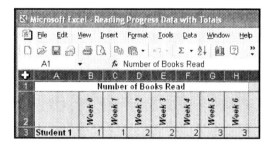
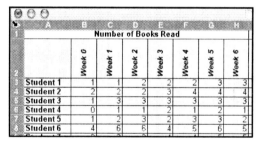

17. Click the **Font Size** list arrow on the Formatting toolbar.

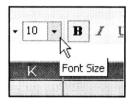
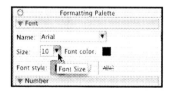

18. Change the font size from the default setting of 10 points to **12 points**.

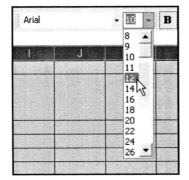

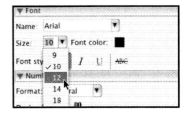

19. Click **File** on the Menu bar.

20. Click **Print Preview**.

—or—

21. Click the **Print Preview** button on the Standard toolbar.

22. Check to make sure that the entire worksheet is still showing on one page. If, due to resizing the font, the worksheet has expanded to two pages, reduce the font size to 11 points and recheck the worksheet.

23. When you are finished checking the worksheet, click on the **Close** button to leave the Print Preview and return to the normal worksheet view.

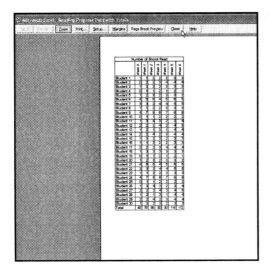

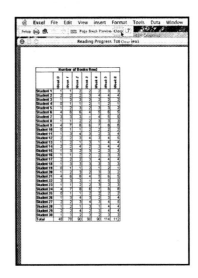

24. At the normal worksheet view, click in any blank cell to remove the highlighting and view the formatting changes you've made.

Adjusting the Column Width

25. Notice that when the font size was increased, the text in column A became wider than the default width. In order to widen the column, move your cursor between column headings A and B. When the cursor changes to a resizing arrow, double click the mouse and the column width will automatically adjust for the font change.

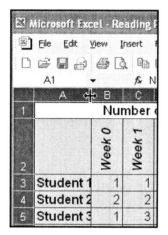
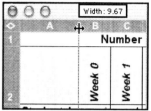

Renaming the Worksheet

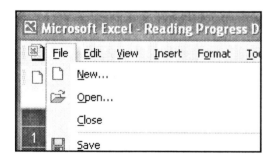

Now that your worksheet is finished, rename it to match the title of your worksheet—**Number of Books Read**.

26. Click **File** on the Menu bar.

27. Click **Save As**.

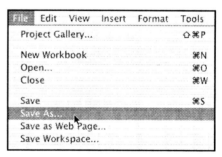

28. At the Save As window, click the **Save in** list arrow and navigate to the folder where you want to save your file.

29. Click in the **File name** textbox and change the file name from **Reading Progress Data with Totals** to **Number of Books Read**.

30. Then click on the **Save** button.

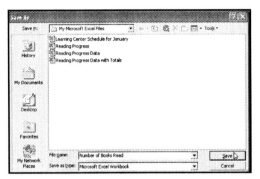 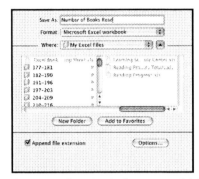

You would think that after all those formatting changes the worksheet would be ready to print. However, there are a few more changes to make in the next activity.

If you need to stop working now, close your worksheet and exit *Excel*. If you can continue, that's great!

Closing the Workbook and Exiting *Microsoft Excel*

31. To close your workbook, click **File** on the Menu bar.

32. Click **Close**.

 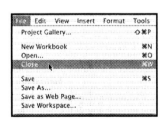

—or—

33. Click the **Close Window** button for the workbook.

34. Exit *Microsoft Excel*.

 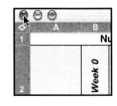

Activity 15—Centering and Setting the Print Area

In this activity you'll take one more look at your worksheet to see how it will look when printed. You'll center the worksheet—both vertically and horizontally—and set the print area before printing.

Getting Started

1. Open the **Number of Books Read** workbook that you worked on in Activity 14, if it is not already open.

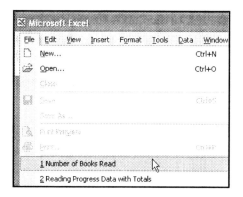 

Note: To open your **Number of Books Read** workbook, click **File** on the Menu bar. You may see your workbook file listed. If so, simply click on the file to open it. If not, click **Open**.

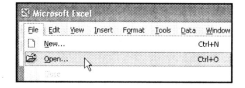 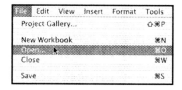

(You can also click the **Open** button on the Standard toolbar.) At the Open window, click the **Look in** list arrow and navigate to where you saved the workbook. Then click the **Number of Books Read** workbook file to select it. Click **Open**.

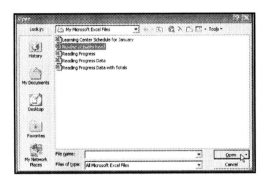

Previewing the Worksheet

Preview your worksheet to see what other changes need to be made prior to printing.

2. Click **File** on the Menu bar.

3. Click **Print Preview**.

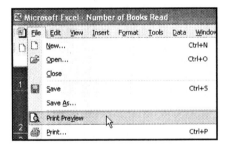
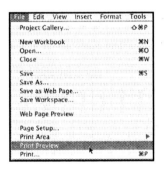

—or—

4. Click the **Print Preview** button on the Standard toolbar.

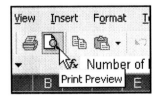
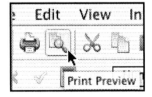

Examine your worksheet and notice how it is left aligned. The worksheet is also resting closer to the top than to the bottom. The worksheet would look much nicer on the printed page if it were centered both vertically and horizontally.

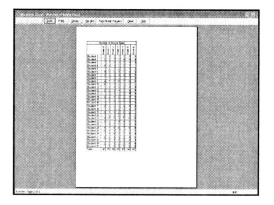 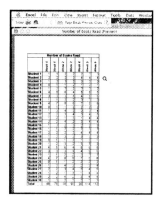

Centering the Worksheet on the Printed Page

5. Click on the **Setup** button above the print preview.

6. At the **Page Setup** window, click on the **Margins** tab to bring it to the forefront.

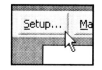

7. Under the **Center on page** option, click the boxes for **Horizontally** and **Vertically**.

8. Then click **OK**.

The worksheet should now be centered both vertically and horizontally on the page.

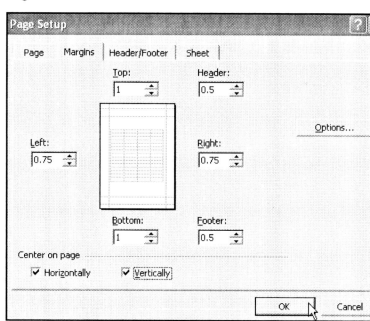

Setting the Print Area for the Worksheet

Although you can tell by the print preview that *Microsoft Excel* only plans to print the worksheet you created, it is always a good idea to set the print area, establishing exactly what cells you do and do not want printed. This is especially important if you only want to print a select portion of a very large worksheet or actually have two or more sets of data on one worksheet.

9. So, click on the **Close** button to leave the Print Preview and return to the normal worksheet view.

10. Scroll down until you see the very last data cell in your worksheet—cell **H33**.

11. Click in cell **H33** and drag to the left and up until all the cells in your worksheet are highlighted. (Yes, all the way from cell **H33** to cell **A1**!) When you hit the top of your screen, keep dragging. As long as you keep pushing up and to the left, the worksheet will automatically scroll up and over for you.

If you don't succeed in highlighting the entire worksheet the first time, simply scroll down to cell H33 and try again.

Note: It is always easier to set the print area from the last data cell to the first data cell because you have more control. The left and top edges of the worksheet help confine the scrolling. If you highlight from cell A1 to H33, there is a greater chance that you will scroll beyond the confines of the worksheet unless you are a very sophisticated mouse user.

Number of Books Read

	Week 0	Week 1	Week 2	Week 3	Week 4	Week 5	Week 6
Student 1	1	1	2	2	2	3	3
Student 2	2	2	2	3	4	4	4
Student 3	1	3	3	3	3	3	3
Student 4	0	1	1	2	1	2	1
Student 5	1	2	3	2	3	3	2
Student 6	4	6	6	4	5	6	5
Student 7	3	3	3	4	4	5	5
Student 8	1	1	2	2	3	3	3
Student 9	4	7	8	6	7	8	8
Student 10	0	1	1	2	2	2	2
Student 11	1	3	4	3	2	3	4
Student 12	2	2	3	4	3	4	5
Student 13	1	2	1	3	1	4	4
Student 14	2	2	4	2	3	4	4
Student 15	1	3	2	3	2	3	3
Student 16	1	1	2	2	2	3	3
Student 17	2	2	2	3	4	4	4
Student 18	1	3	3	3	3	3	3
Student 19	0	1	1	2	1	2	1
Student 20	1	2	3	2	3	3	2
Student 21	4	6	6	4	5	6	5
Student 22	3	3	3	4	4	5	5
Student 23	1	1	2	2	3	3	3
Student 24	4	7	8	6	7	8	8
Student 25	0	1	1	2	2	2	2
Student 26	1	3	4	3	2	3	4
Student 27	2	2	3	4	3	4	5
Student 28	1	2	1	3	1	4	4
Student 29	2	2	4	2	3	4	4
Student 30	1	3	2	3	2	3	3
Total	48	78	90	90	90	114	112

12. Once cells **H33 through A1** are highlighted, click **File** on the Menu bar.
13. Click **Print Area.**
14. Click **Set Print Area.**
15. Click in any empty cell to remove the highlighting.

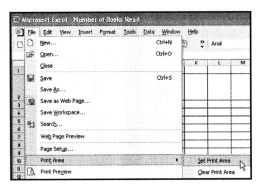 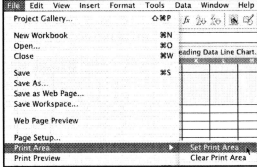

Renaming and Saving the Workbook

Before printing, it is always a good idea to save your work—just in case something happens.

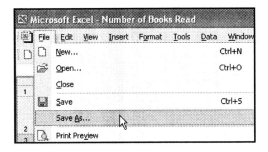 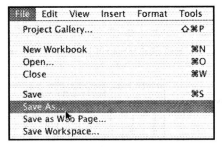

16. Click **File** on the Menu bar.

17. Click **Save As**.

18. At the Save As window, click in the **File name** textbox and change the file name from Number of Books Read to **Number of Books Read Final**.

19. Click **Save**.

Printing the Worksheet

Finally, you're ready to print your worksheet.

20. Click **File** on the Menu bar.

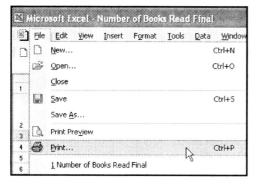 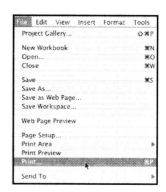

21. Click **Print**.

—or—

22. Click the **Print** button on the Standard toolbar.

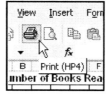 

Closing the Workbook and Exiting Excel

23. To close your workbook, click File on the Menu bar.

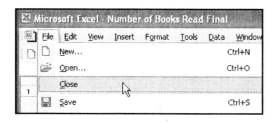 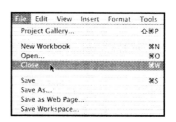

24. Click **Close**.

—or—

25. Click the **Close Window** button for the workbook.

26. Exit *Microsoft Excel*.

 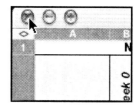

Activity 16—Using Chart Wizard to Create a Column Chart

In this activity you'll create a column chart from the data in your worksheet. Along the way, you'll view all the types of charts *Microsoft Excel* can display, select a chart type, experiment with lots of chart features, place a chart, name a chart, and print a chart. Have fun!

Getting Started

1. Open the **Number of Books Read Final** workbook that you worked on in **Activity 15**, if it is not already open.

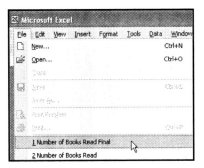 

Note: To open your **Number of Books Read Final** workbook, click **File** on the Menu bar. You may see your workbook file listed. If so, simply click on the file to open it. If not, click **Open**.

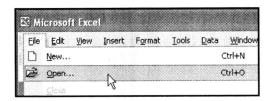 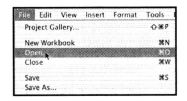

(You can also click the **Open** button on the Standard toolbar.)

At the Open window, click the **Look in** list arrow and navigate to where you saved the workbook. Then click the **Number of Books Read Final** workbook file to select it. Click **Open**.

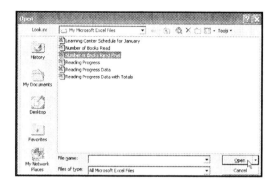 

Before telling *Microsoft Excel* to create a chart from your worksheet, take some time to think about what you actually want charted. It is best to keep your chart simple, conveying select information based upon what you intend to display or show. In this case, you want to show the principal that your students have successfully increased the number of books read over the past six weeks.

Keeping the rule of simplicity in mind, is it best to display all thirty of the students' number of books read over the last six weeks or just the **Total** row?

Check the box that indicates your decision.

❑ all thirty students' number of books read

❑ just the **Total** row

If you selected "just the **Total** row," you're right.

Aside from the **Total** row, you'll also need to display the column labels (Week 0, Week 1, Week 2, etc.), so the principal can see the totals for each week.

So, which two rows from your worksheet will you tell *Microsoft Excel* to chart?

If you selected rows **2** and **33**, you're right!

Selecting Multiple Rows of Data for Charting

First, select the rows that you want charted.

2. Click on the **row heading 2** to select (highlight) the entire row.

3. Scroll down the worksheet until **row 33** appears.

4. Hold down the **Control** key (**Command [⌘]** key on the Mac) on your keyboard and click on the **row heading 33**.

Note: Holding down the Control key allows you to select multiple nonadjacent rows. If you simply clicked on the row 33 heading without holding down the Control key on your keyboard, you lost your selection of row 2. Remember that you want <u>both</u> rows charted, so scroll back up and try again. Click on row heading 2. Then scroll down, hold down the Control key, and select row heading 33.

5. Check your selection. Scroll up and down, making sure that both row **2** and row **33** are selected before proceeding.

Using the Chart Wizard

6. To tell *Microsoft Excel* that you want these rows charted, click **Insert** on the Menu bar.

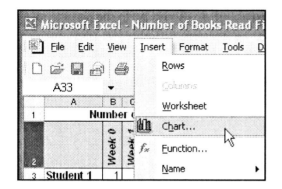 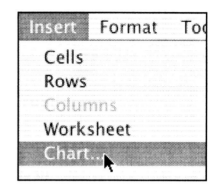

7. Click **Chart**.

—or—

8. Click the **Chart Wizard** button on the Standard toolbar.

A Chart Wizard dialog box appears. There are several things to examine before proceeding.

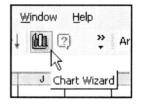 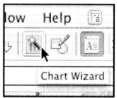

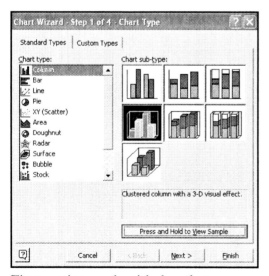 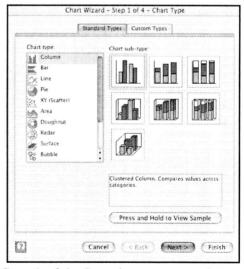

First, notice on the title bar that you are on Step 1 of 4. So, when you complete your selection at this window, there are three more to go.

Second, notice on the title bar that the focus of this window is the selection of the Chart Type. So, this is where you find the most appropriate type of chart for the data you plan to display.

There are fourteen Standard Types of charts (Column, Bar, Line, Pie, etc.) and twenty Custom Types of charts (Black and White Line, Black and White Pie, etc.).

9. Click on the **Standard Types** tab to bring it to the forefront, if necessary.

Each of the Standard Types has several Chart Sub-Types. For example, the Columns chart (which is the default selection) has seven sub-types.

Viewing Charts

10. Single click on the **Bar chart**. It has six sub-types.

Note: If you double click by mistake, it takes you to Step 2. Simply click on the Back button to return to Step 1.

11. Single click on each sub-type and read its description.
12. Continue exploring the Chart Wizard – Chart Type window in this manner until you've examined all of the Standard Types of charts.
13. Then click on the **Custom Types** tab to bring it to the forefront.
14. Single click on each Chart Type to see how the data is displayed. Rather than displaying several chart sub-types, an actual Sample of the Chart Type is displayed using the data that you selected on the worksheet.

Selecting a Chart Type

15. When you are done exploring, click on the **Standard Types** tab to bring it to the forefront.
16. Under Chart Type, single click on the **Column** chart.
17. Under Chart Sub-Type, single click on the first sub-type in the second row—the **Clustered column with a 3-D visual effect.**

Previewing a Sample Chart

18. Click on the **Press and hold to view sample** button to see what this type of chart will look like displaying the data you selected.

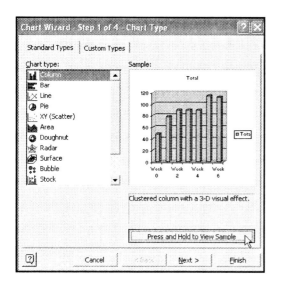
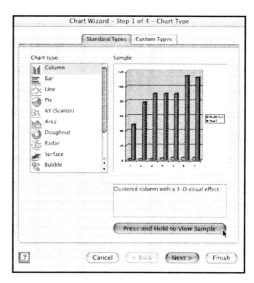

19. That's all for Step 1. So click on the **Next** button to go on to Step 2.

Examining Data Ranges and Series Settings

20. At the Chart Wizard—Step 2 of 4—Chart Source Data dialog box, *Microsoft Excel* provides you with an opportunity to change the Data Range or the Series that you have selected for the chart. Since you don't have to make any changes, click on the **Next** button to go on to Step 3.

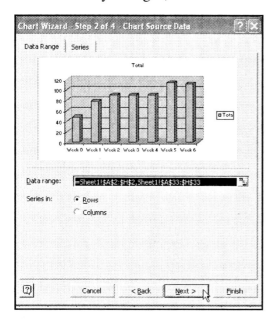
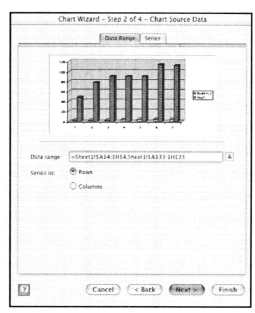

21. At the Chart Wizard – Step 3 of 4 – Chart Options dialog box, notice that there are several tabs to explore. Click the **Titles** tab to bring it to the forefront, if necessary.

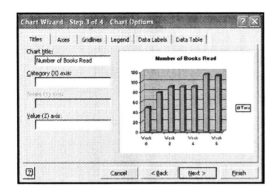 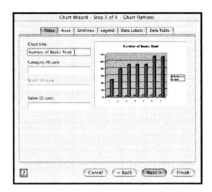

Adding a Chart Title

The Titles tab provides you with the opportunity to change the chart title, the label for the X axis, Y axis, and Z axis. You can see that the title definitely needs changing. Total is an inappropriate title for this chart.

22. Click in the **Chart title** textbox and type the following:
    Number of Books Read

Within a few seconds, the chart will display the new title. Did you see that?

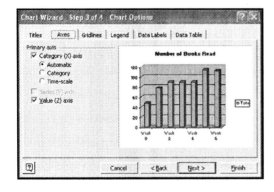 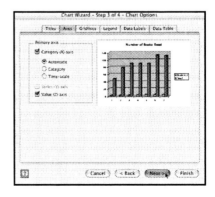

Experimenting with Axes Labels

23. Click on the **Axes** tab to bring it to the forefront.

24. You can remove Week 0, Week 1, Week 2, etc., from the X axis by clicking on the Category (X) Axis to deselect it. Try it! Notice that the weeks have disappeared.

25. Of course, you want the weeks back. So, click on the Category (X) Axis again to restore Week 0, Week 1, Week 2, etc.

26. Similarly, you can remove the numbers 0, 20, 40, etc. from the Z axis by clicking on the Value (Z) Axis to deselect it. Try it! Notice that the numbers have disappeared.

27. Of course, you want the numbers back. So, click on the Category (Z) Axis again to restore the numbers 0, 20, 40, etc.

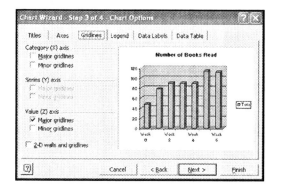 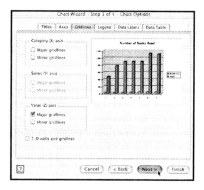

Experimenting with Gridlines

28. Click on the **Gridlines** tab to bring it to the forefront.

29. Notice that the **Value (Z) Axis—Major Gridlines** is the only type of gridline that is selected and display. Try the other types of gridlines by selecting and then deselecting them. Watch how they change your chart.

30. When you are done experimenting with the other types of gridlines, make sure that the **Value (Z) Axis—Major Gridlines** is the only type of gridline that is selected and displayed.

Moving and Removing the Legend

31. Click on the **Legends** tab to bring it to the forefront.

32. The legend is currently displayed on the right side of the chart. Change the position of the legend by clicking on other **Placements**, such as Bottom, Corner, Top, and Left.

33. When you are done viewing the legend in a variety of placements, click on **Show Legend** to deselect it. The legend will disappear. You really don't need a legend with this simple chart.

Adding Data Labels

34. Click on the **Data Labels** tab to bring it to the forefront.

    (Notice that the default setting is **None** on the Mac.) No data labels are showing on your chart. However, it is helpful to include data labels that display the values of the columns.

35. Click on **Value (Show Value** on the Mac). The numbers that represent the values of the columns are now displayed.

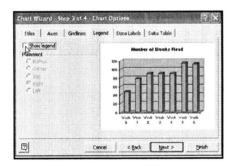
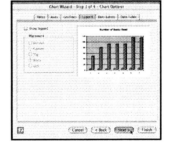

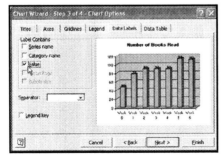
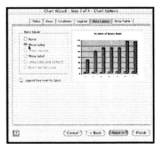

Experimenting with Data Tables

36. Click on the **Data Table** tab to bring it to the forefront.
37. Click on **Show Data Table**, so you can see what your chart looks like with a data table added to the bottom.
38. Click on **Show Data Table** again to deselect it.

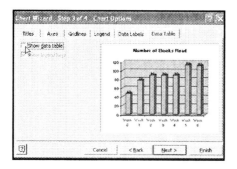 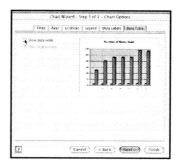

39. Well, that's all the tabs for Step 3. Click the **Next** button to go on to Step 4.

Placing the Chart

At the Chart Wizard – Step 4 – Chart Location dialog box, you have two options. The default selection is for your chart to become an object on the worksheet where your data is stored. The second option is for your chart to become a new sheet in the workbook with its own name.

40. Click **As new sheet**.

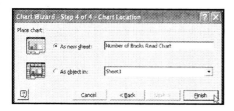 

Naming the Chart

41. Click in the **As new sheet** textbox and type the following: **Number of Books Read Chart**

42. Click the **Finish** button.

Your chart is now the first tab in your workbook.

Printing the Chart

43. To print your **Number of Books Read Chart**, click **File** on the Menu bar.

44. Click **Print**.

—or—

45. Click the **Print** button on the Standard toolbar.

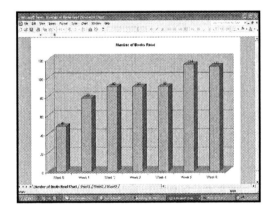

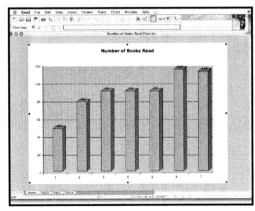

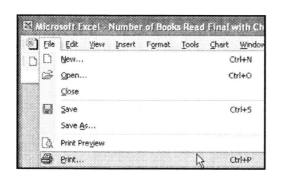

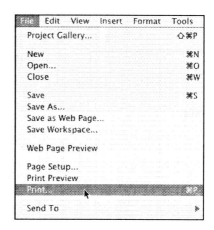

Returning to the Worksheet

46. Click on the **Sheet1** tab to return to your original worksheet.

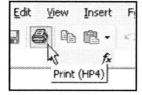

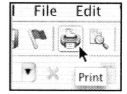

47. Click in any empty cell to remove the highlighting from rows 2 and 33.

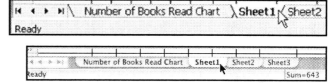

Renaming the Workbook

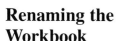

48. To rename your workbook, click **File** on the Menu bar.

49. Click **Save As**.

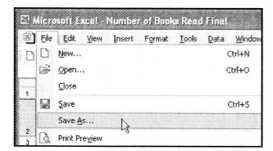

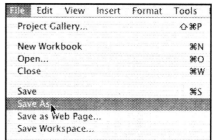

50. At the Save As window, click in the **File name** textbox and change the file name from **Number of Books Read Final** to **Number of Books Read with Chart**.

51. Then click the **Save** button.

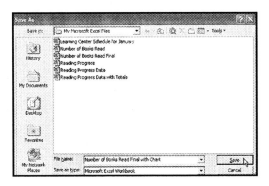 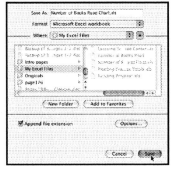

Closing the Workbook and Exiting Excel

52. To close your workbook, click **File** on the Menu bar.

53. Click **Close**.

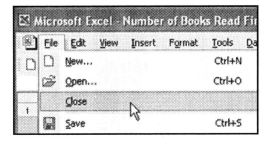 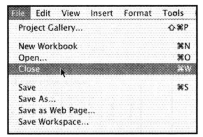

—or—

54. Click the **Close Window** button for the workbook.

55. Exit *Microsoft Excel*.

 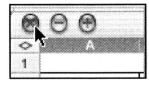

Activity 17—Renaming, Moving, and Deleting Worksheets

In this activity, you will rename your worksheets, reorder your worksheets by moving them, and delete the worksheets that you are not using in your workbook. You'll be amazed at how simple it is to rename, move, and delete worksheets. Let's get started!

Getting Started

1. Open **Number of Books Read with Chart** workbook that you worked on in **Activity 16**, if it is not already open.

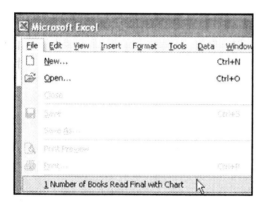 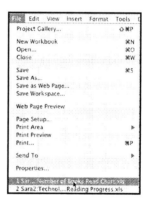

Note: To open your **Number of Books Read with Chart** workbook, click **File** on the Menu bar. You may see your workbook file listed. If so, simply click on the file to open it. If not, click **Open**. (You can also click the **Open** button on the Standard toolbar.)

 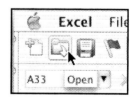

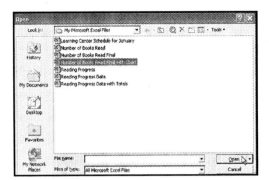 

At the Open window, click the **Look in** list arrow and navigate to where you saved the workbook. Then click the **Number of Books Read with Chart** workbook file to select it. Click **Open**.

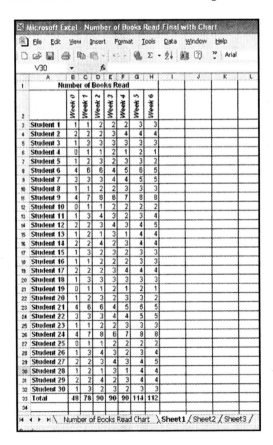 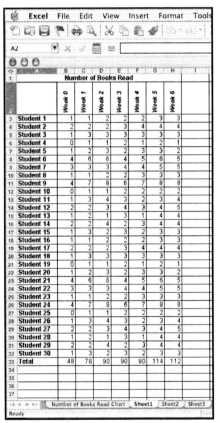

	Week 0	Week 1	Week 2	Week 3	Week 4	Week 5	Week 6
Student 1	1	1	2	2	2	3	3
Student 2	2	2	2	3	4	4	4
Student 3	1	3	3	3	3	3	3
Student 4	0	1	1	2	1	2	1
Student 5	1	2	3	2	3	3	2
Student 6	4	6	6	4	5	6	5
Student 7	3	3	3	4	4	5	5
Student 8	1	1	2	2	3	3	3
Student 9	4	7	8	6	7	8	8
Student 10	0	1	1	2	2	2	2
Student 11	1	3	4	3	2	3	4
Student 12	2	2	3	4	3	4	5
Student 13	1	2	1	3	1	4	4
Student 14	2	2	4	2	3	4	4
Student 15	1	3	2	3	2	3	3
Student 16	1	1	2	2	2	3	3
Student 17	2	2	2	3	4	4	4
Student 18	1	3	3	3	3	3	3
Student 19	0	1	1	2	1	2	1
Student 20	1	2	3	2	3	3	2
Student 21	4	6	6	4	5	6	5
Student 22	3	3	3	4	4	5	5
Student 23	1	1	2	2	3	3	3
Student 24	4	7	8	6	7	8	8
Student 25	0	1	1	2	2	2	2
Student 26	1	3	4	3	2	3	4
Student 27	2	2	3	4	3	4	5
Student 28	1	2	1	3	1	4	4
Student 29	2	2	4	2	3	4	4
Student 30	1	3	2	3	2	3	3
Total	48	78	90	90	90	114	112

Notice that the **Number of Books Read** worksheet (**Sheet1**) appears. It was the worksheet at the forefront when you closed your file after the last activity.

Examine the tabs at the bottom of the worksheet. The active worksheet is
Sheet1, where you entered the data for the number of books read.

Renaming Worksheets within a Workbook

Rename this tab to something more meaningful than Sheet1.

2. Click **Format** on the Menu bar.

3. Click **Sheet**.

4. Click **Rename**.

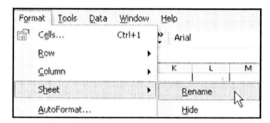 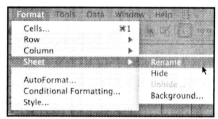

—or—

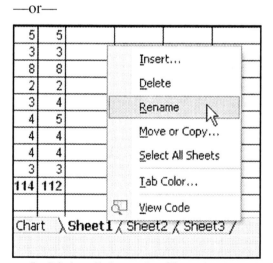 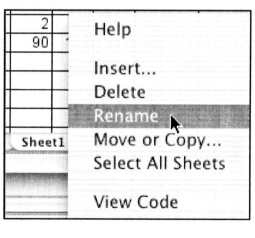

5. Right-click on the **Sheet1** tab and select **Rename** from the pop-up menu.
   (If you are working on a Mac, you will have to hold down the **Control** key
   as you click.)

Notice that the **Sheet1** tab is now
highlighted, awaiting your changes.

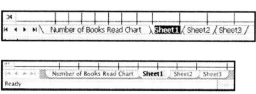

6. Type the following: **Reading Data**

Notice that as you begin typing, **Sheet1** disappears and **Reading Data** fills the tab.

7. Click on the **Number of Books Read Chart** tab to bring the chart to the forefront.

8. Give this tab a simpler name. Click **Format** on the Menu bar.

9. Click **Sheet**.

10. Click **Rename**.

—or—

11. Right-click on the **Number of Books Read Chart** tab and select **Rename** from the pop-up menu. (If you are using a Mac, hold down the Control key as you click.)

Notice that the **Number of Books Read Chart** tab is now highlighted, awaiting your changes.

12. Type the following: **Reading Chart**

Notice that as you begin typing, **Number of Books Read Chart** disappears and **Reading Chart** fills the tab.

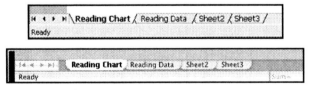

Moving Worksheets in the Workbook

Reorder the worksheets in your workbook by placing the Reading Data worksheet before the Reading Chart worksheet.

13. In order to move the Reading Data worksheet, click on the **Reading Data** tab and hold down the mouse button until a white page symbol appears.

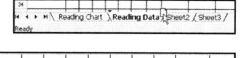

14. Continue to hold down the mouse button and drag the white page symbol to the left, dropping it to the left of the Reading Chart tab.

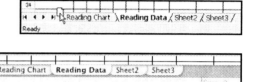

Notice that Reading Data is now the first tab and Reading Chart is now the second tab in your workbook.

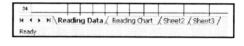

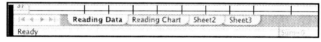

Deleting Worksheets

Since you will not be using Sheet2 and Sheet3 within this workbook, delete them.

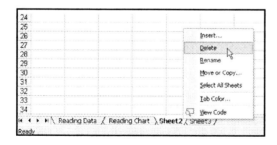

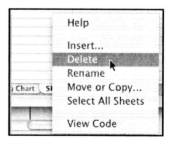

15. Right click on the **Sheet2** tab and select **Delete** from the pop-up menu. (If you are using a Mac, hold down the **Control** key as you click.)

—or—

16. Click **Edit** on the Menu bar.

17. Click **Delete Sheet**.

18. A warning message will appear, asking if you really want to delete this worksheet. Since you do, click on the **OK** button.

19. See if you can remove **Sheet3** on your own. If not, just repeat the above steps, substituting Sheet3 for Sheet2 in the directions.

Saving and Renaming the Workbook

20. To save and rename your book, click **File** on the Menu bar.

21. Click **Save As**.

22. At the Save As window, click in the **File name** textbox and change the file name from **Number of Books Read with Chart** to **Reading Data and Chart**.

23. Then click on the **Save** button.

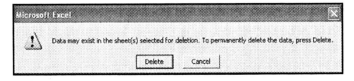

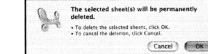

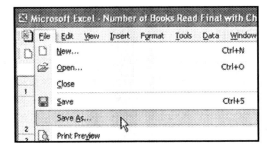 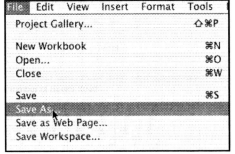

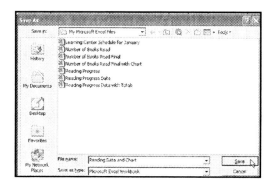

Closing the Workbook and Exiting Microsoft Excel

24. To close your workbook, click **File** on the Menu bar.

25. Click **Close**.

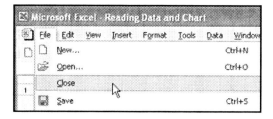
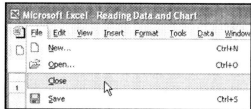

—or—

26. Click on the **Close Window** button for the workbook.

27. Exit *Microsoft Excel*.

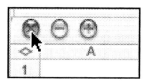

Activity 18—Adding a Worksheet to a Workbook and Moving Data from One Worksheet to Another

In this activity, you will add a worksheet to your workbook and move data from one worksheet to another in preparation for creating a special line chart with a data table for your principal.

Getting Started

1. Open the **Reading Data and Chart** workbook that you worked on in **Activity 17**, if it is not already open.

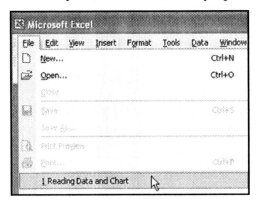 

Note: To open your **Reading Data and Chart** workbook, click **File** on the Menu bar. You may see your workbook file listed. If so, simply click on the file to open it. If not, click **Open**. (You can also click the **Open** button on the Standard toolbar.)

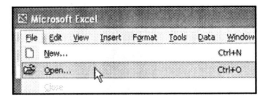 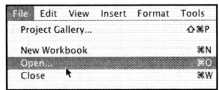

At the Open window, click the **Look in** list arrow and navigate to where you saved the workbook. Then click the **Reading Data and Chart** workbook file to select it. Click **Open**.

 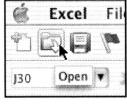

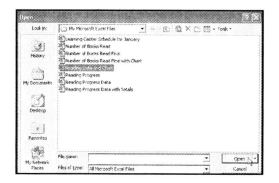 

Adding a Worksheet to the Workbook

2. To add a worksheet to your workbook, click **Insert** on the Menu bar.

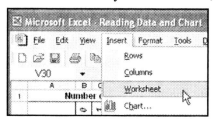 

3. Click **Worksheet**.

Moving and Renaming the New Worksheet

4. To move the new worksheet, click on the **Sheet1** tab and drag it to the right of the Reading Chart tab, making it the third worksheet in your workbook.

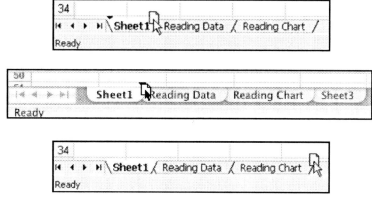

5. Rename the new worksheet **Principal's Chart**.

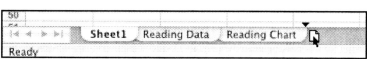

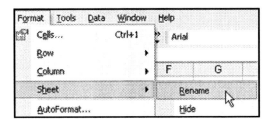 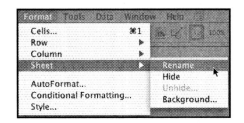

Note: If you don't remember how to rename the worksheet, here's how. Click **Format** on the Menu bar. Click **Sheet**. Then click **Rename**. Alternatively, right-click)or control-click if you are working on a Mac) on the **Sheet1** tab and select **Rename** from the pop-up menu. The **Sheet1** tab is now highlighted, awaiting your changes. Type the following: **Principal's Chart**. Press the **Enter** or **Return** key on your keyboard.

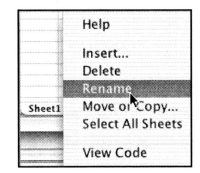

Copying and Pasting Data from One Worksheet to Another

First you will copy the data you need for the principal's special line chart from the Reading Data worksheet. Then you will paste the data into the Principal's Chart worksheet. Ready?

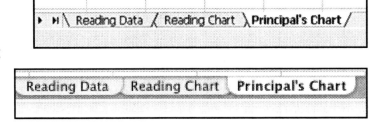

6. Click on the **Reading Data** tab to bring this worksheet to the forefront.

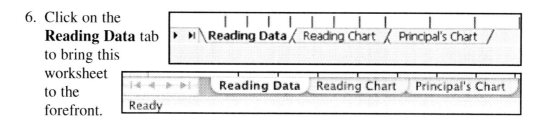

Which two rows of data do you need to copy from this worksheet to the Principal's Chart worksheet in order to create the special line chart?

The two rows of data that need to be copied are _____ and _____.

If you selected rows 2 and 33, you're right! You need row 2 because it has the labels. You need row 33 because it has the total number of books read each week.

In addition, you'll copy row 1, as it has the worksheet title.

7. Multiple-select rows 1, 2, and 33.

Note: If you don't remember how to select multiple rows, here's how. Hold down the **Control** key on your keyboard (Command [⌘] key on a Mac) and click on **the row headings 1, 2, and 33**. Be sure that you don't drag when selecting row headings 1 and 2. If you do, you will get an error message when trying to copy the selection. Rather, click on **row heading 1** to select it. Hold down the **Control** (or ⌘) key and click on **row heading 2** to select it. Then scroll down until you see row 33. Hold down the **Control** (or ⌘) key and click on **row heading 33**.

After making sure that only rows 1, 2, and 33 have been selected, copy these rows.

8. Click **Edit** on the Menu bar.

9. Click **Copy**.

—or—

10. Click the **Copy** button on the Standard toolbar.

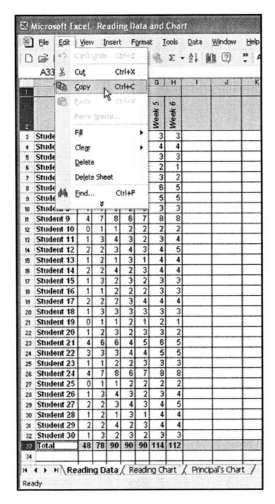

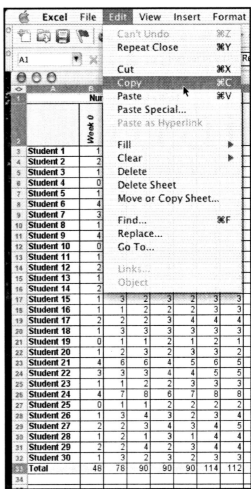

11. Click on the **Principal's Chart** tab to bring this worksheet to the forefront.

12. Click in cell **A1** to make it the active cell.

Paste the data from the Reading Data worksheet.

13. Click **Edit** on the Menu bar.

14. Click **Paste**.

—or—

15. Click the **Paste** button on the Standard toolbar.

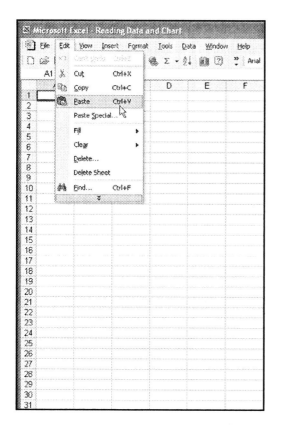
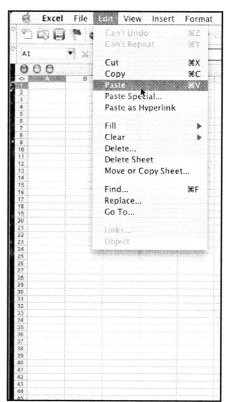

Rows 1, 2, and 33 from the Reading Data worksheet should now appear on the Principal's Chart worksheet in rows 1, 2, and 3.

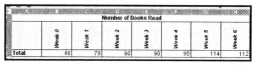

16. Click in any white cell to remove the highlighting from rows 1, 2, and 3.

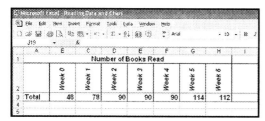

You did it! You added a new worksheet, moved the worksheet, renamed the worksheet, and copied and pasted data from one worksheet to another. Now you are ready to create a special line chart for the principal. You will do so in the next activity.

Saving and Renaming the Workbook

17. To save and rename your workbook, click **File** on the Menu bar.
18. Click **Save As**.
19. At the Save As window, click in the **File name** textbox and change the file name **Reading Data and Chart** to **Reading Data with New Worksheet**. (If you are using a Mac, just change the file name to **Reading Data With New Sheet**.)

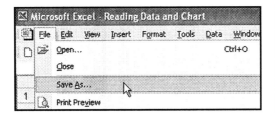 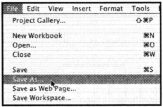

20. Then click the **Save** button.

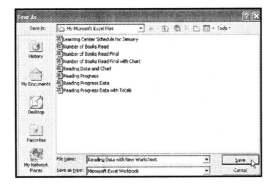 

Go ahead to the next activity or close your workbook file and exit *Microsoft Excel*.

Closing the Workbook and Exiting Microsoft Excel

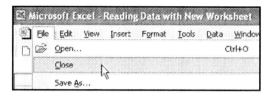 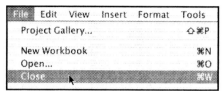

21. To close your workbook, click **File** on the Menu bar.

22. Click **Close**.

—or—

23. Click the **Close Window** button for the workbook.

24. Exit *Microsoft Excel*.

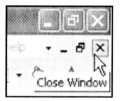 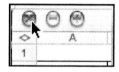

Activity 19—Creating a Line Chart with a Data Table

In this activity, you will create a special line chart with a data table for your principal. The line chart will display your students' reading progress—proof that a pizza party is in order for your class.

Getting Started

1. Open the **Reading Data with New Worksheet workbook** that you worked on in **Activity 18**, if it is not already open.

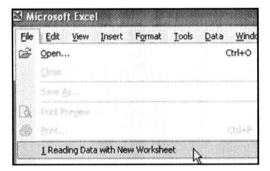 

Note: To open the **Reading Data with New Worksheet** workbook, click **File** on the Menu bar. You may see your workbook file listed. If so, simply click on the file to open it. If not, click **Open**.

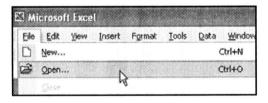 

 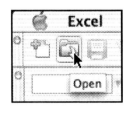

(You can also click the **Open** button on the Standard toolbar.) At the Open window, click the **Look in** list arrow and navigate to where you saved the workbook. Then click the **Reading Data with New Worksheet** workbook file to select it. Click **Open**.

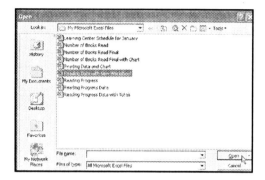

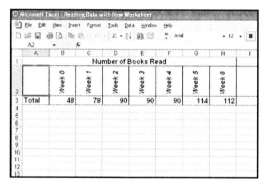
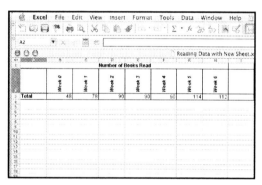

Selecting Data for the Line Chart

In order to create a special line chart for the principal, it is necessary to select the data that should be charted, just like you did for the 3-D column chart.

2. Click in cell **H3** and drag left and up to cell **A2**.

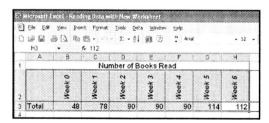
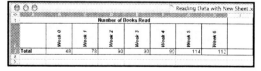

Note: If you make a mistake while trying to select cells A2 through H3, simply click in any white cell to deselect what you've highlighted and try again.

Creating a Line Chart

3. Once cells **A2 through H3** are selected, click **Insert** on the Menu bar.

4. Click **Chart.**

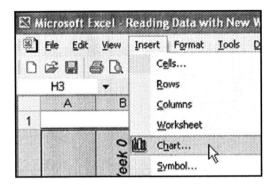 

—or—

5. Click on the **Chart Wizard** button on the Standard toolbar.

6. At the **Chart Wizard – Step 1 of 4 – Chart Type** dialog box,

 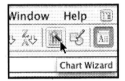

click the **Standard Types** tab to bring it to the forefront, if necessary.

7. Under Chart type, click **Line.**

8. Under Chart sub-type, select the **Line chart with markers displayed at each data value**—the first line chart in the second row.

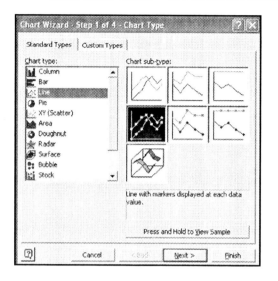
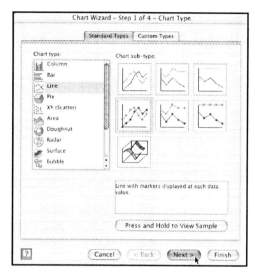

9. Click and hold on the **Press and hold to view sample** button to preview your special line chart. (If you are a Mac user, don't panic at what you see. You will adjust the display at the next Chart Wizard screen.)

10. Release the mouse button when you are finished viewing the sample line chart.

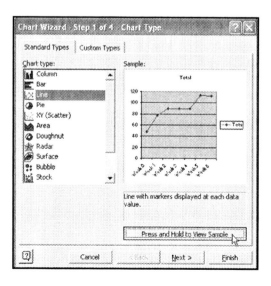
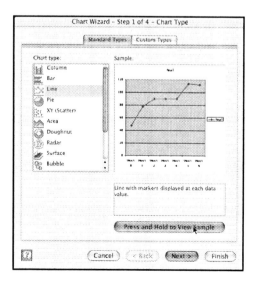

11. Click on the Next button to view the **Chart Wizard – Step 2 of 4 – Chart Source Data** dialog box. (If you are a Mac user, click **Rows** and then click **Next**. This will change your display.)

12. Since you do not need to change the data range for this chart, click the **Next** button to view the **Chart Wizard – Step 3 of 4 – Chart Options** dialog box.

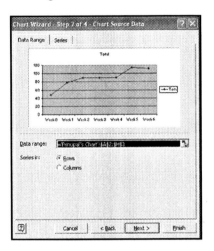 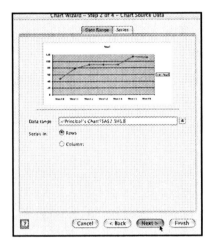

At the **Chart Wizard – Step 3 of 4 – Chart Options** window, there are several changes to make.

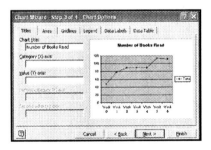 

13. First, click the **Titles** tab to bring it to the forefront, if necessary.

14. Then click in the **Chart title textbox** and type the following: **Number of Books Read**

15. Click the **Legend** tab to bring it to the forefront.

16. Deselect **Show legend** to remove the Total box from your chart.

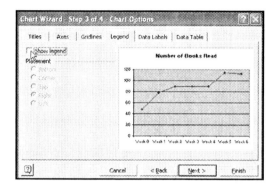 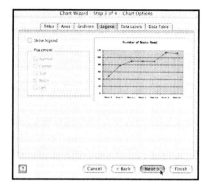

17. Click on the **Data Table** tab to bring it to the forefront.

18. Click on **Show data table**.

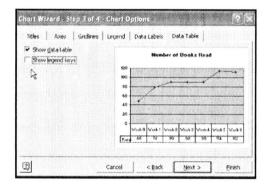 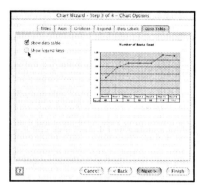

Notice that when you selected **Show data table**, the **Show legend keys** automatically became selected as well.

19. Since this is unnecessary for interpreting the chart, click on **Show legend keys** to deselect it.

20. That's it for this window. So, click on the **Next** button to view the **Chart Wizard – Step 4 of 4 – Chart Location** dialog box.

21. At the **Chart Wizard – Step 4 of 4 – Chart Location** dialog box, the default selection is to place the chart as an object in the Principal's Chart worksheet rather than as its own worksheet as you did before. Click on the **Finish** button to accept this selection.

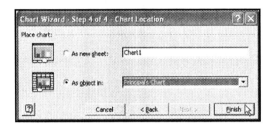 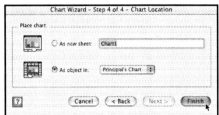

Notice that the chart has been placed as an object in the Principal's Chart worksheet.

Moving the Chart in a Worksheet

Move the chart, centering it below the data rows.

22. Move your cursor over a white area on the chart, avoiding the text, numbers, plot area, and data table area. When the Chart Area flag appears, hold down your mouse button until your cursor changes to the move symbol (a four-way arrow on the PC and a hand on the Mac).

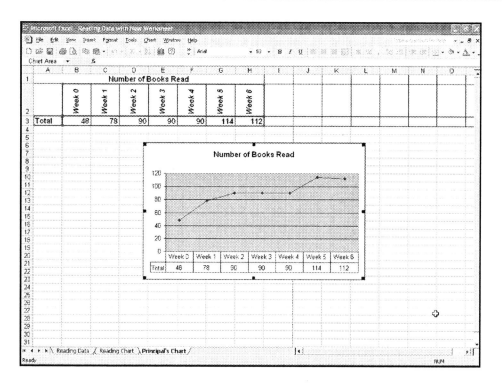

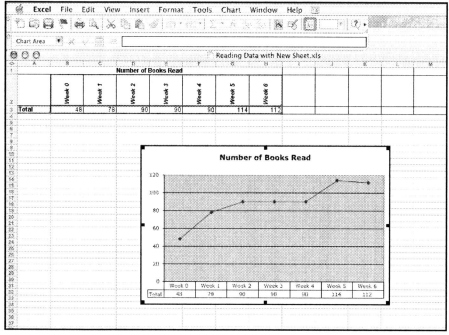

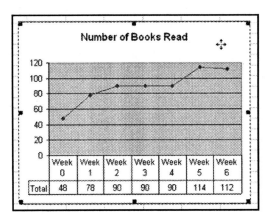
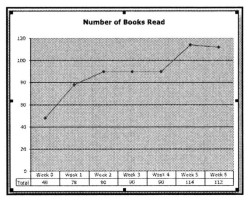

23. Drag the chart to the left, below the worksheet data area. Try to center the chart as best you can.

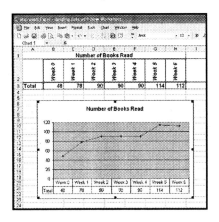
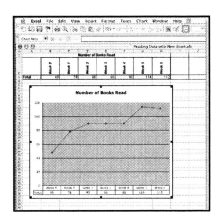

Previewing the Line Chart with a Data Table Before Printing

24. Click any white area on the chart to select the entire chart for printing.
25. Click **File** on the Menu bar.
26. Click **Print Preview**.

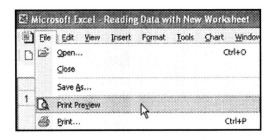

—or—

27. Click the **Print Preview** button on the Standard toolbar.

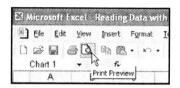 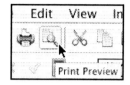

Printing from Print Preview

Rather than closing the Print Preview and printing from the worksheet, you can print from this area.

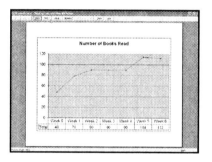 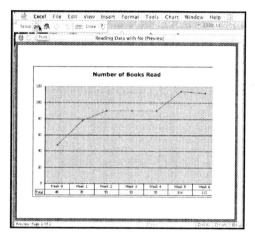

28. Click the **Print** button.

29. At the **Print** dialog box, notice that the **Selected Chart** will be printed, as that is the portion of the worksheetyou selected.

30. Click **OK** or **Print**.

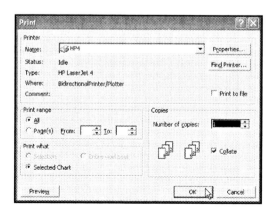 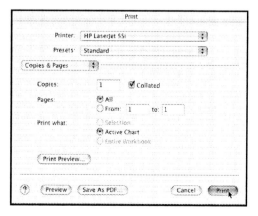

After printing, you will automatically be returned to your worksheet. Ready to save it?

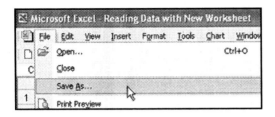 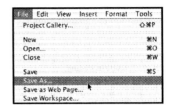

Saving and Renaming the Workbook

31. To save and rename your workbook, click **File** on the Menu bar.

32. Click **Save As**.

33. At the Save As window, click in the **File name** textbox and change the file name from **Reading Data with New Worksheet** to **Reading Data with Principal's Chart** (or just **Reading Data Principal** if you are using a Mac).

34. Click **Save**.

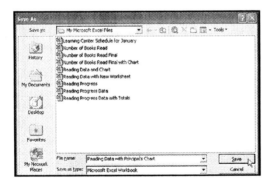 

Feel free to continue with the next activity. You will learn how to add a background to the line chart. However, if you are ready to take a break, close your workbook and exit *Microsoft Excel*.

Closing the Workbook and Exiting *Microsoft Excel*

35. To close your workbook, click **File** on the Menu bar.

36. Click **Close**.

—or—

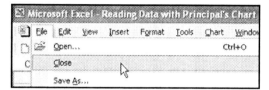 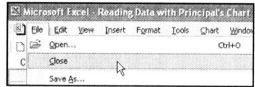

37. Click the **Close** button on the Standard toolbar.

38. Exit *Microsoft Excel*.

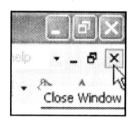 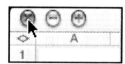

Activity 20—Adding a Background Picture to a Chart

Want to really impress your principal? In this activity, you will add a background picture to the **Number of Books Read** chart! Ready to get started?

Getting Started

1. Open the **Reading Data with Principal's Chart** workbook that you worked on in **Activity 19**, if it is not already open.

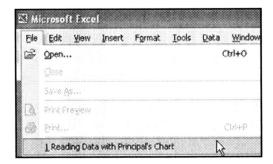 

Note: To open the **Reading Data with Principal's Chart** workbook, click **File** on the Menu bar. You may see your workbook file listed. If so, simply click on the file to open it. If not, click **Open**.

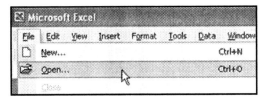 

(You can also click the Open button on the Standard toolbar.) At the Open window, click the **Look in** list arrow and navigate to where you saved the workbook.

Then click the **Reading Data with Principal's Chart** workbook file to select it.
Click **Open**.

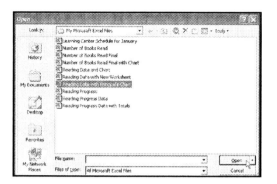

Adding a Background Picture to the Chart

It's fun to add a background picture to a chart. It's also fast and easy. Prior to
adding the picture, however, you must have one in mind and in digital format.
For the Number of Books Read chart, you will place a picture of a book in the
background. Don't worry! There is a picture file on the CD in the back of this
book just for this activity. However, if you have your own digital picture of a
book, feel free to use it. Ready to get started?

2. Place the CD from the back of this book into the CD drive of your
   computer system.

3. Double-click on the
   plot area of your line
   chart. Be sure not to
   click on any lines or
   markers.

4. When you do, a
   Format Plot Area
   dialog box appears.
   Click the **Fill Effects**
   button.

5. When you do, a Fill
   Effect dialog box
   appears. Click the
   Picture tab to bring it
   to the forefront.

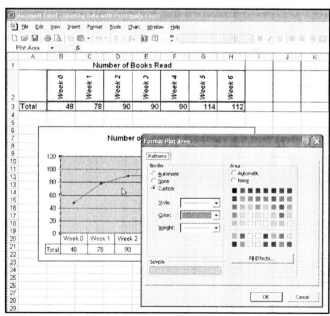

6. Then click the **Select Picture** button.

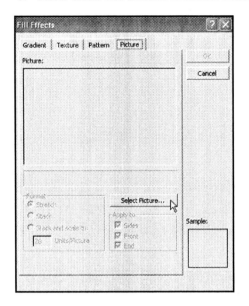 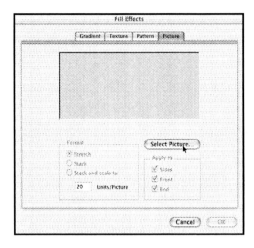

7. At the **Select Picture** dialog box, click on the **Look in** list arrow and navigate to the CD drive of your computer system.

8. Click the **Book** picture file to select it.

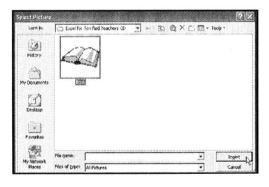 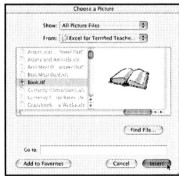

9. Click the **Insert** button.
10. You will return to the **Fill Effects** dialog box. Click OK.

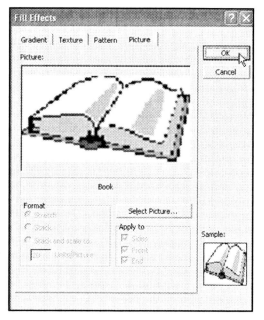

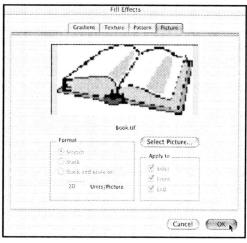

11. You will return to the **Format Plot Area** dialog box. Notice that the picture of the book is displayed in the **Sample** area, although somewhat distortedly. Click **OK**.

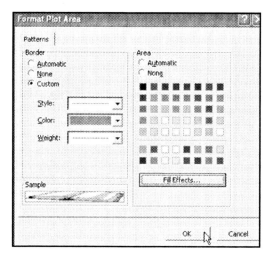

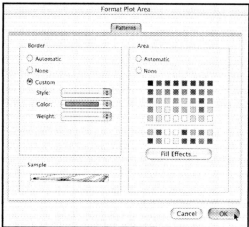

The picture of a book now appears behind your line chart. The data line and markers are somewhat difficult to see, however. The data line can be made thicker, so that it stands out more. The data markers can be made larger and of a contrasting color, so that they stand out more as well. It just takes a few clicks and some simple formatting.

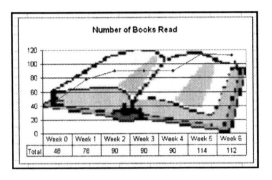
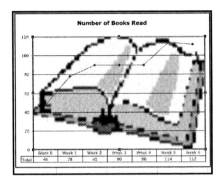

12. Double click on the **data line**.

13. When you do, a **Format Data Series** dialog box appears. Click the **Patterns** tab to bring it to the forefront, if necessary. You will make several changes here.

14. Under **Line**, click the **Weight** list arrow and select the thickest line displayed. (It is the last one.)

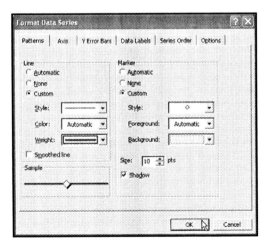
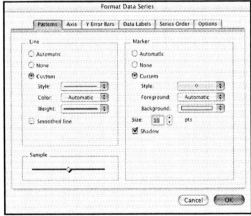

Note: Notice that as you make changes to your data line and markers, the changes are automatically displayed in the **Sample** area.

15. Under **Marker/Size**, click the up arrow until you reach **10 points**.
16. Under **Marker**, click **Shadow** to select it.
17. Under **Marker**, click the **Background** list arrow and select a bright, contrasting color, such as **yellow**.
18. Then click **OK**. When you return to your worksheet and chart, examine the changes you made. Much better looking, eh?

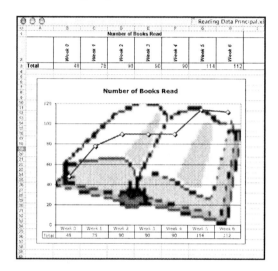
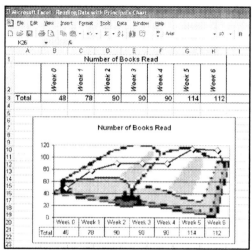

Saving and Renaming the Workbook

19. To save and rename your workbook, click **File** on the Menu bar.

20. Click **Save As**.

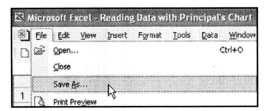 

21. At the **Save As** window, click in the **File name** textbox and change the file name from **Reading Data with Principal's Chart** to **Reading Data with Principal's Line Chart**. (or just **Reading Data Line Chart** if you are using a Mac.)

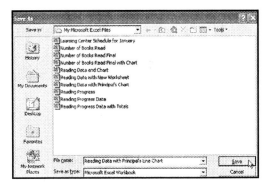 

22. Click **Save**.

In the next activity you will see how to copy and paste the line chart into a memorandum composed in *Microsoft Word*. So, move onto Activity 21 or close your workbook file and exit *Microsoft Excel*.

Closing the Workbook and Exiting *Microsoft Excel*

23. To close your workbook, click **File** on the Menu bar.

24. Click **Close**.

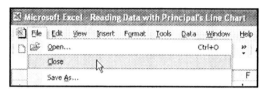 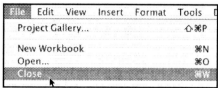

—or—

25. Click the **Close Window** button on the Standard toolbar.

 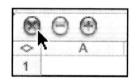

26. Then exit *Microsoft Excel*.

Activity 21—Integrating a *Microsoft Excel* Chart into *Microsoft Word*

In this activity, you will write a memorandum to the principal, telling her that your students have doubled their reading over the past six weeks. Of course, you'll want to copy that special line chart into the document to add a clear visual display of your students' progress.

Getting Started

1. Open **Reading Data with Principal's Line Chart** workbook that you worked on in **Activity 20**, if it is not already open.

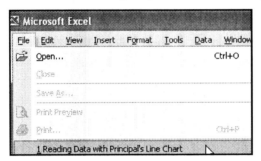 

Note: To open the Reading **Data with Principal's Line Chart** workbook, click **File** on the Menu bar. You may see your workbook file listed. If so, simply click on the file to open it. If not, click **Open**.

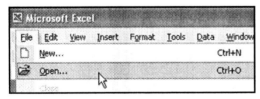 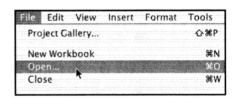

(You can also click the **Open** windowon the Standard toolbar.) At the Open window, click the **Look in** list arrow and navigate to where you saved the workbook. Then click the **Reading Data with Principal's Line Chart** workbook file to select it. Click **Open**.

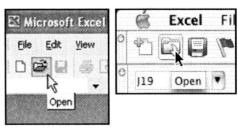

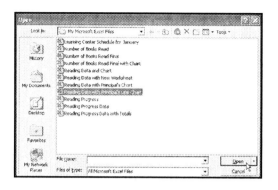 

2. When the worksheet appears, click the **Principal's Chart tab** to bring the worksheet and chart to the forefront, if necessary.

3. Click on the **Number of Books Read** line chart to select it.

4. Click **File** on the Menu bar.

5. Click **Copy**.

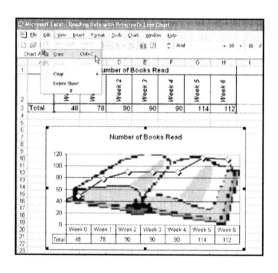 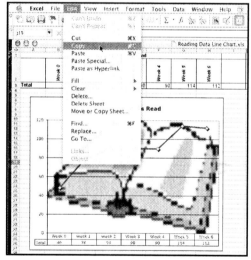

Opening *Microsoft Word* on a PC

To open *Microsoft Word*, click the **Start** button on the Task bar. Click *Microsoft Word*.

Note: If you don't see *Microsoft Word* right away, click **All Programs**. *Microsoft Word* will appear by itself within the All Programs menu or within the *Microsoft Office Suite* folder.

Opening *Microsoft Word* on a Mac

To open *Microsoft Word* on a Mac, hide *Microsoft Excel* first, so you can see your desktop. Then double-click on your Mac hard drive icon to open it. Double-click the *Microsoft Office X* folder. Double-click the *Microsoft Word* program icon to launch it. At the Project Gallery window, notice that *Microsoft Word* is already selected for you. So, simply click OK.

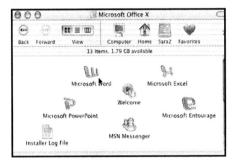

Note: When *Microsoft Word* opens on the Mac, you may need to display the Standard toolbar and the Formatting toolbar, if they do not already appear on your screen. To do so, click **View** on the Menu bar, click **Toolbars**, and then select **Standard**. Repeat this process to display the **Formatting** toolbar as well.

Opening a *Microsoft Word* Document

The **Reading Progress Memorandum** file that you need to complete this activity is on the CD in the back of this book.

6. To obtain the file you need, place the CD in the CD drive of your computer system.

7. Click **File** on the Menu bar.

8. Click **Open**.

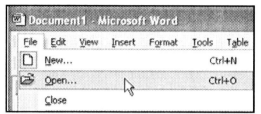 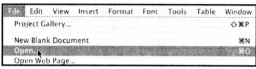

—or—

9. Click the **Open** button on the Standard toolbar.

10. At the Open window, click the **Look in** list arrow and navigate to the CD drive on your computer system.

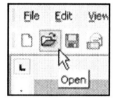 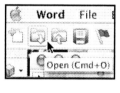

11. Click the **Reading Progress Memorandum** file to select it.

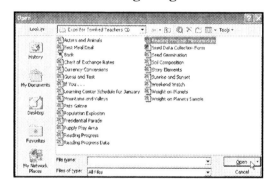 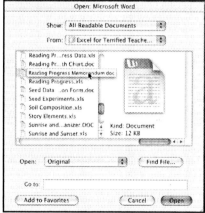

12. Click **Open**.

Preparing to Insert the Chart

13. When the **Reading Progress Memorandum** appears on your screen, click below the text.

I am happy to let you know that my students have doubled their reading over the past six weeks. The chart shows their progress. We are all looking forward to the pizza party!

|

14. Leave at least one empty line between the text and your cursor. If you don't see one line space, press the **Enter** or **Return** key on your keyboard one time.

Note: Notice that your cursor is flush left. When you paste the chart into the **Reading Progress Memorandum**, you want it centered.

15. Click the **Center** button on the Formatting toolbar. Watch your cursor jump to the center.

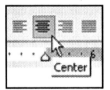
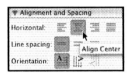

Inserting the Chart into the Memorandum

16. To paste the line chart into the **Reading Progress Memorandum**, click **Edit** on the Menu bar.

17. Click **Paste**.

—or—

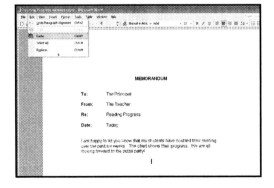
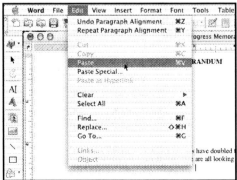

18. Click the **Paste** button on the Standard toolbar.

 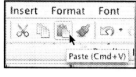

Note: If you wish to take the time to personalize the **Reading Progress Memorandum** by changing the principal's name, the teacher's name, and the date, feel free to do so.

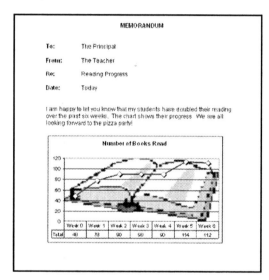 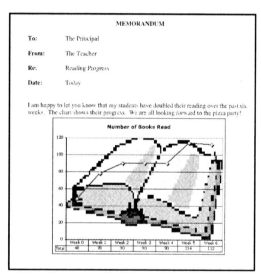

Printing the Completed Memorandum

Now that you **Reading Progress Memorandum** is complete, print it.

19. Click **File** on the Menu bar.
20. Click **Print**.

—or—

21. Click the **Print** button on the Standard toolbar.

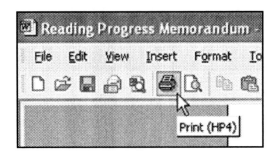 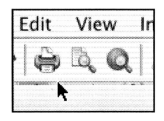

22. At the Print window, click **OK** or **Print**.

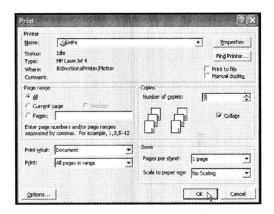 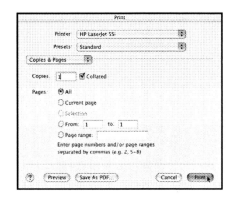

Saving and Renaming the Memorandum

23. To save and rename your memorandum, click **File** on the Menu bar.

24. Click **Save As**.

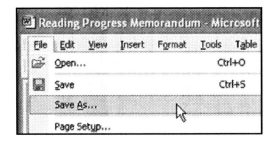 

25. At the Save As window, click in the **File name** textbox and change the file name from **Reading Progress Memorandum** to **Reading Progress Memorandum with Chart**. (On the Mac, due to character limitations, you may need to shorten the file name to something like **Reading Progress Memo Chart**.)

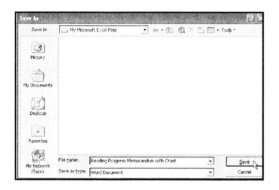 

26. Click the **Save in** list arrow and navigate to where you want to save your file.

27. Then click on the **Save** button.

Closing the Memorandum and Exiting the *Microsoft Word* Program

28. To close the **Reading Progress Memorandum with Chart** file, click **File** on the Menu bar.

29. Click **Close**.

—or—

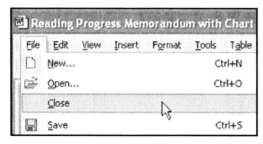 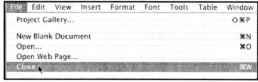

30. Click the **Close Window** button.

31. Exit *Microsoft Word* just as you exit *Microsoft Excel*.

Closing the Workbook and Exiting Microsoft Excel

Now that you have closed *Microsoft Word*, close *Microsoft Excel* as well.

Note: If you are using a PC, you will automatically be taken back to *Microsoft Excel*. If you are using a Mac, you will need to unhide *Microsoft Excel*.

 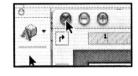

32. To close the **Reading Data with Principal's Line Chart** workbook, click File on the Menu bar.

33. Click **Close**.

—or—

34. Click the **Close Window** button.

35. Exit *Microsoft Excel*.

Well, since your students are entitled to a pizza party, in the next activity you will create a pie chart that displays their favorite types of pizza pie.

Activity 22—Creating a Pie Chart

Congratulations! Your class is getting a pizza party. All you have to do is decide which kind of pizza your students want. In this activity, you will create a pie chart that displays your students' favorite pizzas. So, collect some data, enter some data, and create a pizza pie chart!

Getting Started

1. Open a new *Microsoft Excel* workbook.
2. Click in cell **B1** and type the following: **Pepperoni Pizza**
3. Press the Tab key to move to cell **C1** and type the following: **Cheese Pizza**
4. Press the Tab key to move to cell **D1** and type the following: **Veggie Pizza**
5. Press the Tab key to move to cell **E1** and type the following: **Deluxe Pizza**

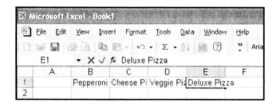 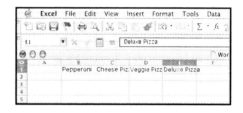

Wrapping Text within a Cell

Notice how the text in each of the cells is cut off. For example, you can't read the entire Pepperoni Pizza or Cheese Pizza headings. Of course, you could widen the columns. However, if you don't want the columns to be wider, but you do want your headings to show, wrap the text. It's easy to do. Here's how.

6. Click on the row **label 1** to select the entire row.
7. Click on the **Format** menu and select **Cells**.

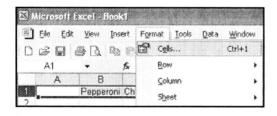 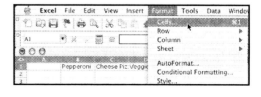

8. At the **Format Cells** window, click the **Alignment** tab to bring it to the forefront.

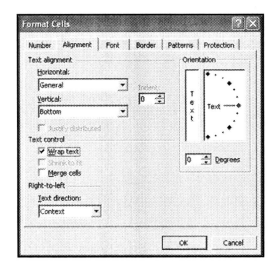 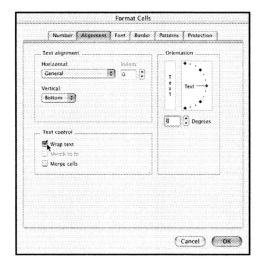

9. Under the **Text control menu**, click on **Wrap text**.

10. Then click on the **OK** button to return to your worksheet.

11. While row 1 is still selected, click on the **Bold** button on the Formatting toolbar.

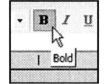 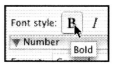

12. Click the **Center** button on the Formatting toolbar as well.

13. If you are working on a PC, notice that the word Pepperoni is split between two lines because it is wider than the default column width setting. In order

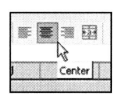 

to widen the column, move your cursor between the column headings B and C. When your cursor changes to a resizing symbol (two-headed arrow), click and drag column B wider—just wide enough so that Pepperoni is on the top line.

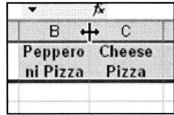

14. Click in cell **A2** and type the following: **Students**

15. Click in cell **B2** and type the following: **16**

16. Click in cell **C2** and type the following: **6**

17. Click in cell **D2** and type the following: **4**

18. Click in cell **E2** and type the following: **4**

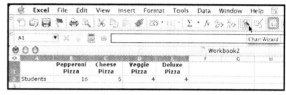

Selecting the Data for Charting

19. Select (highlight) cells **A1 through E2**.

Note: If you have difficulty selecting cells A2 through E3, simply click in any empty cell and try again.

20. Once cells A1 through E2 are selected, click the **Chart Wizard** button on the Standard toolbar.

21. At the Chart Wizard – Step 1 of 4 – Chart Type dialog box, click on the **Standard Types** tab to bring it to the forefront, if necessary.

22. Under Chart type, select **Pie**.

23. Under Chart subtype, select the **Exploded pie with a 3-D visual effect**— the second pie chart in the second row.

24. If you want, click and hold on the **Press and hold to view sample** button to preview the pie chart.

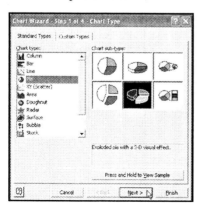
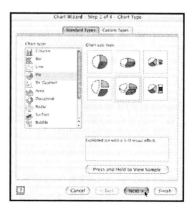

25. Click on the **Next** button to view the Chart Wizard – Step 2 of 4 – Chart Source Data dialog box.

26. Since you do not need to change the data rage for this chart, click the **Next** button to view the Chart Wizard – Step 3 of 4 – Chart Options dialog box.

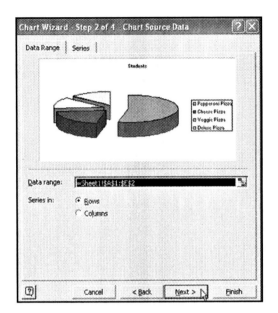
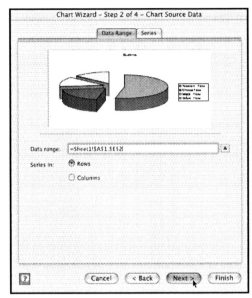

At the Chart Wizard – Step 3 of 4 – Chart Options window, there are several changes to make.

27. Click the **Titles** tab to bring it to the forefront, if necessary.

28. Click in the **Chart title** textbox and type the following: **Our Favorite Pizzas**.

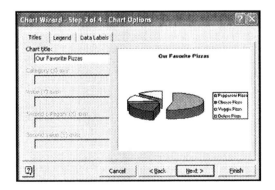
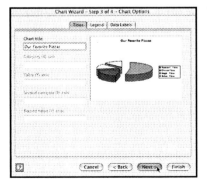

29. Click the **Legends** tab to bring it to the forefront.

30. Click **Show Legend** to deselect it. The legend disappears from your display.

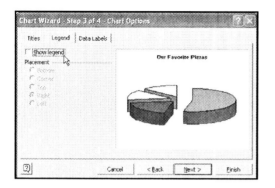 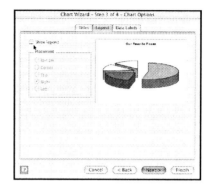

Note: Don't worry, you'll show this information in another way through the Data Labels.

31. Click the **Data Labels** tab, to bring it to the forefront.

32. Under the **Label Contains** menu, click **Category name**.

33. Then click **Percentage**.

Note: If you are using a Mac, click **Show label and percent**.

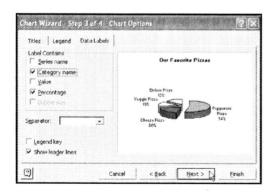 

34. That's it for Step 3 of 4. So, click on the **Next** button to view the Chart Wizard – Step 4 of 4 – Chart Location dialog box.

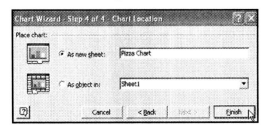 

35. At the Chart Wizard – Step 4 of 4 – Chart Location dialog box, click **As new sheet**.

36. Click in the **As new sheet** textbox and type the following: **Pizza Chart**

37. Then click the **Finish** button.

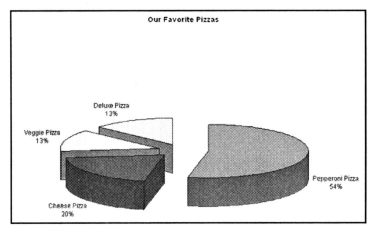

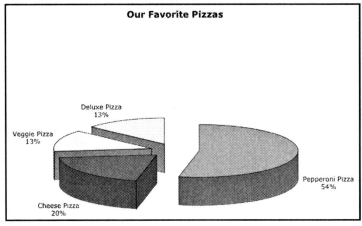

Printing the Pizza Chart

38. To print your pizza chart, click **File** on the Menu bar.
39. Click **Print**.

—or—

40. Click the **Print** button on the Standard toolbar.

Saving the Workbook

41. To save your workbook, click **File** on the Menu bar.
42. Click **Save**.

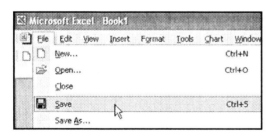 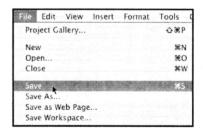

—or—

43. Click the **Save** button on the Standard toolbar.

 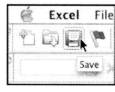

44. At the Save As window, click the **Save in** list arrow and navigate to where you want to save your workbook file.

45. Click in the **File name** textbox and change the file name from **Book1** to **Pizza Data and Chart**.

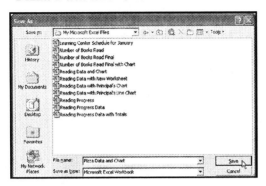 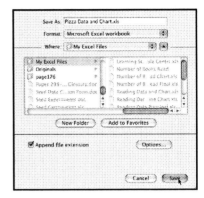

46. Then click the **Save** button.

Closing the Workbook and Exiting Microsoft Excel

47. To close your workbook, click **File** on the Menu bar.

48. Click **Close**.

—or—

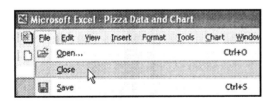 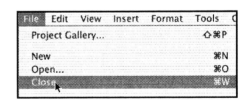

49. Click the **Window Close** button.

50. Exit *Microsoft Excel*.

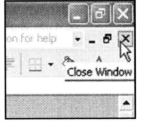 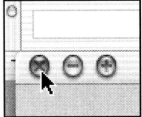

Activity 23—Using Relative and Absolute Formulas in an Electronic Gradebook

An electronic gradebook is one of the most popular uses of a spreadsheet or workbook. In this activity, you will create a gradebook template and set up formulas with relative and absolute references. Then in the next activity you will use the electronic gradebook for recording and calculating students' grades.

Getting Started
1. Launch *Microsoft Excel* to start a new workbook.

Creating a Stacked Vertical Column Label

You've learned how to create standard and horizontal column labels. Now it's time to learn one more type—a stacked vertical column label. It's so easy!

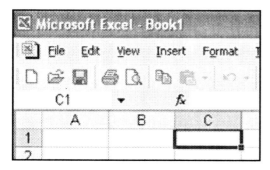

2. Click in cell **C1** to select it.
3. Click **Format** on the Menu bar.
4. Click **Cells**.

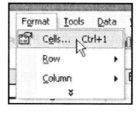
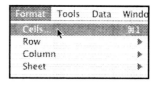

5. At the **Format Cells** window, click the **Alignment** tab to bring it to the forefront.

6. Under Orientation, click on the stacked vertical **Text**.

7. Then click **OK** to return to your worksheet.

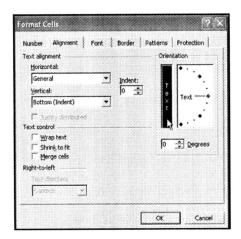 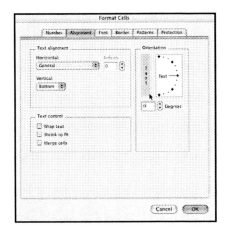

8. Remaining in cell **C1**, type the following: **Assignment 1**

9. Click the **Enter** box to the left of the formula bar.

Notice that you now have a stacked vertical column label—Assignment 1.

Using AutoFill to Extend the Stacked Vertical Column Label

Use the AutoFill feature to extend the column label from Assignment 1 through Assignment 5.

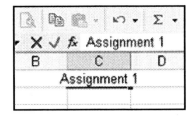

10. Using your mouse, point to the fill handle—the small square at the bottom-right corner of the active cell (C1). When the cell pointer is positioned on the fill handle, it changes to a black cross. Click when you see the black cross and drag the fill handle to the right, highlighting cells **D1 through G1**.

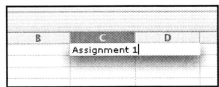

11. Release the mouse button. Assignment 2 through Assignment 5 automatically appears.

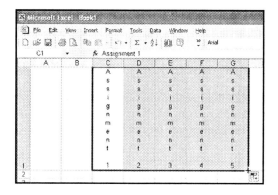
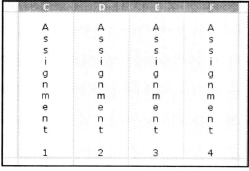

Resizing the Stacked Vertical Column Labels

These columns are wider than necessary. So, resize them!

12. While the Assignment 1 through Assignment 5 labels are still selected, click **Format** on the Menu bar.

13. Click **Column**.

14. Click **Width**.

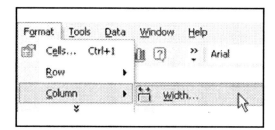
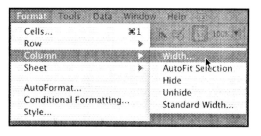

15. At the **Column Width** dialog box, change the column width from the default setting to 5.

16. Then click **OK**.

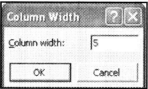
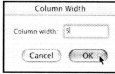

Adding Other Column Labels

17. Click in cell I1 and type the following: **Total**
18. Click in cell J1 and type the following: **Percent**

Changing from Stacked Vertical Column Labels to Horizontal Labels

Note that both of these column labels are stacked. Change them back to normal.

19. Select (highlight) the **Total** and the **Percent** column labels (cells **I1 and J1**).
20. Click **Format** on the Menu bar.
21. Click **Cells**.

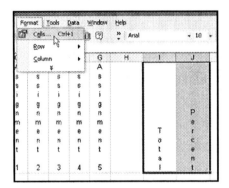
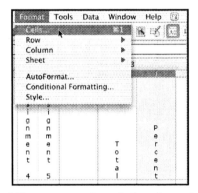

22. At the **Format Cells** dialog box, click the **Alignment** tab to bring it to the forefront.
23. Under **Orientation**, click the stacked **Text** to deselect it.
24. Click **OK**. The two column labels are now horizontal.

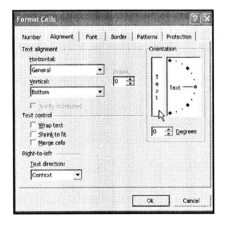
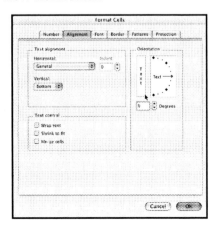

Creating a Cell Label with Wrapped Text

25. Click in cell **A2** and type the following: **Name**

26. Click in cell **B2** and type the following: **Possible Points**

27. Press the **Tab** key on your keyboard to move to cell **C2**.

Notice that Possible Points is cut off. Rather than widen the column, wrap the text.

28. Click in cell **B2**.

29. Click **Format** on the Menu bar.

30. Click **Cells**.

 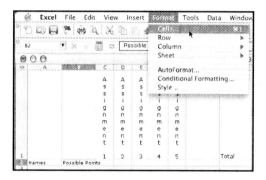

31. At the **Format Cells** dialog box, click the **Alignment** tab to bring it to the forefront.

32. Under **Text control**, click **Wrap text**.

33. Then click **OK**.

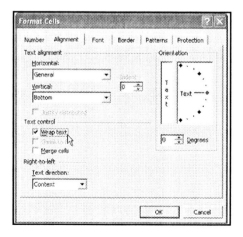 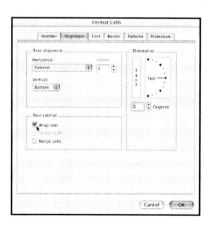

Setting Up the Total Formula

Ready to insert some formulas? They only take a minute, and they save you lots of time calculating student grades. Here goes!

34. Click in cell **I2** to select it. In this cell, you will be entering a formula that totals the students' possible points on assignments 1 through 5.

Before entering the total formula, you need to clearly understand what cells you want to add up. So, after examining your workbook, can you identify the five cells that will contribute to the total? If you answered cells C2, D2, E2, F2, and G2, you're right!

35. Remaining in cell I2, click the **AutoSum** button on the Standard toolbar.

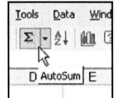 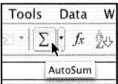

Notice that in cell I2 and in the formula bar, a partial formula, called the SUM function, appears **=SUM()**. Your cursor is flashing within the parentheses, as the SUM function is awaiting your input. It will carry out the addition of any series or range of cells you enter.

36. Since you want cells C2 through G2 to be added, click in cell **C2** and drag through cell **G2** to select this range.

When cells C2 through G2 are selected, the SUM function completes its formula. Can you see **=SUM(C2:G2)** in cell I2 and in the formula bar?

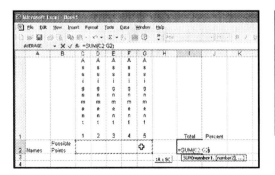 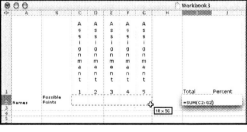

Note: Remember that the colon (:) in the formula indicates a range. In this case, the colon indicates the range of cells from C2 through G2, which includes D2, E2, and F2.

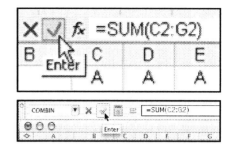

37. In order to accept this formula, click the **Enter** button to the left of the formula bar.

Note: Don't be alarmed that the Total in cell I2 is zero (0). You haven't entered values for the possible points for each assignment yet. Later, when you do, the 0 will change, reflecting the total of the values you enter.

Using a Relative Reference with AutoFill

You've already used a relative reference with a formula in a previous activity. You just didn't know it! Now it's time to understand what relative reference means because soon you'll be using its alternative—an absolute reference.

When a relative reference is used, *Microsoft Excel* copies a formula from one cell and places it in another cell relative to the original cell. Sound confusing? Well, here's an example right out of your current worksheet. The Total formula in cell I2 is =SUM(C2:G2). It sums the values in cells C2 through G2. If the formula was copied to cell I3, you wouldn't want the exact same values (C2:G2) added. Rather, you would want the values relative to this row instead—cell C3 through G3—added. So, when *Microsoft Excel* copies the formula from I2 to I3, it sums the values relative to cells C3 through G3 rather than C2 through G2.

Did you understand that? If so, good going! If not, read it a few more times.

38. Remaining in cell **I2**, use the **AutoFill** feature to copy the formula down through cell **I12**. (For this activity, you'll have only ten students.) Using your mouse, point to the fill handle—the small square at the bottom-right corner of the active cell (I2). When the cell pointer is positioned on the fill handle, it changes to a black cross. Click when you see the black cross and drag the fill handle down, highlighting cells I3 through I12. Release the mouse button. Zeros will automatically appear in all highlighted cells.

			1	2	3	4	5		Total	Percent
1										
2	Names	Possible Points							0	
3									0	
4									0	
5									0	
6									0	
7									0	
8									0	
9									0	
10									0	
11									0	
12									0	
13										
14										

Names	Possible Points	1	2	3	4	5		Total
								0
								0
								0
								0
								0
								0
								0
								0
								0
								0
								0

39. Click in cell **I3**, look at the formula in the formula bar, and notice how it has changed relative to the values added in this row—C3 through G3.

40. Click in cell **I4**, look at the formula in the formula bar, and notice how it has changed relative to the values added in this row—C4 through G4.

Setting Up the Percent Formula

The percent formula will calculate the percent score for each student. Using the percent formula, *Microsoft Excel* will divide the total points earned by the total possible points for all assignments.

41. Click in cell **J3**. This is where the percent score for the first student will be calculated.

42. In order to calculate the percent score for this student, you divide the Total points the student earned (cell I3) by the Total possible points for all assignments (cell I2). So, in cell **J3**, type the formula **=I3/I2**.

43. Then click the **Enter** button to the left of the formula bar.

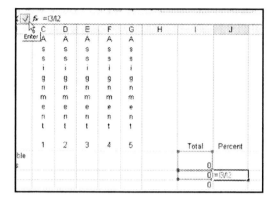

Note: Don't be alarmed when you see the error value message #DIV/0. This is one of seven error messages *Microsoft Excel* displays when it "thinks" there is something wrong with a formula. In this case, the #DIV/0 error value message appears because *Microsoft Excel* doesn't like dividing by zero. The error value message will disappear once the possible points for each assignment and the student scores are entered in the next activity. Remember that you are setting up a template that can be used again and again. You don't want to enter values yet.

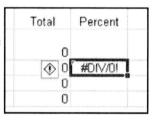

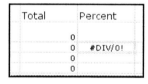

Using an Absolute Reference with AutoFill

44. Click in cell **J3** again and look at the formula **=I3/I2** displayed in the formula bar.

Before using AutoFill to copy the formula =I3/I2 to cells J4 through J12, part of the formula needs to be an Absolute Reference. Cell I2 contains the Total possible points for all assignments. The percent score for your ten students is calculated by using this specific value each and every time. So, the value in cell I2 must remain unchanged when the formula is copied from cell J3 through J12. This makes cell I2 is an Absolute Reference, whereas cell I3 is a Relative Reference.

Did you understand that? If so, good going! If not, read it a few more times.

45. In order to make cell I2 an Absolute Reference, click your cursor immediately after the division sign (/) in the formula bar.

46. Type a **dollar sign ($)** in front of the **I**.

47. Move your cursor after the **I** and type another **dollar sign ($)** in front of the **2**.

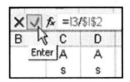 

Just like the equal sign (=) tells *Microsoft Excel* that this is a formula, the dollar sign ($) tells *Microsoft Excel* that this is an Absolute Reference—not to be changed when using AutoFill to copy formulas.

48. Click on the **Enter** button to the left of the formula bar to accept the formula.

49. Remaining in cell **J3**, use the **AutoFill** feature to copy the formula down through cell J12. Using your mouse, point to the fill handle—the small square at the bottom-right corner of the active cell (J3). When the cell pointer is positioned on the fill handle, it changes to a black cross. Click when you see the black cross and drag the fill handle down, highlighting cells **J4 through J12**. Release the mouse button. The #DIV/0 error value message will automatically appear in all highlighted cells.

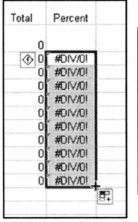

Displaying Cell Values As Percentages

You will recall that the formulas entered in the Percent column were expressed as fractions, such as =I3/I2 and =I4/I2. So, when values are added to the worksheet and the formula results are displayed, they will be expressed in decimal fractions, such as 0.75 and 0.95.

50. In order to express the formula results as percents, click on the **column heading J** to select the entire column.

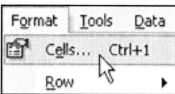

51. Click **Format** on the Menu bar.

52. Click **Cells**.

53. At the Format Cells dialog box, click the **Number** tab to bring it to the forefront, if necessary.

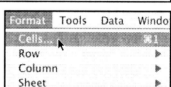

54. Under Category, click on **Percentage**.

55. Then change the **Decimal places** from the default setting of 2 to **0**, so that *Microsoft Excel* does the rounding to the nearest whole percent for you.

56. Then click **OK** to return to your worksheet.

Congratulations! Your gradebook template is complete.

Saving the Gradebook Template

Now that your gradebook template is complete, save it.

57. If you are using a PC, in the Task Pane, click **General Templates**.

58. At the **Save As** dialog window, notice that your file is being placed in the **Templates** folder.

59. Click in the **File name** textbox and type the following: **Gradebook Template**

60. Click **Save**.

61. If you are using a Mac, click **File** on the Menu bar.

62. Click **Save As**.

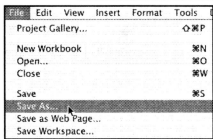

63. At the Save dialog box, click the **Format** list arrow and select **Template**. *Microsoft Excel* will automatically place your file in the **My Templates** folder.

64. Click in the **Name** textbox and type the following: **Gradebook Template**

65. Click **Save**.

Closing the Workbook and Exiting *Microsoft Excel*

66. To close your workbook, click **File** on the Menu bar.

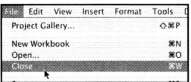

67. Click **Close**.

—or—

68. Click the **Close Window** button.

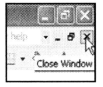
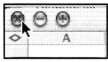

If you're ready, willing, and able, go on to the next activity. If not, exit *Microsoft Excel*.

Activity 24—Using the Gradebook

Boy, this is going to be the easiest activity! Since you've already created the Gradebook Template with all the formulas in place, all you have to do is enter student names and scores. *Microsoft Excel* does the calculations automatically!

Getting Started

Open the **Gradebook Template**.

1. If you are using a PC, in the Task Pane, click **General Templates**.

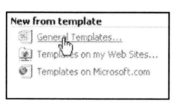 

2. At the Templates dialog window, click the **General** tab to bring it to the forefront, if necessary.

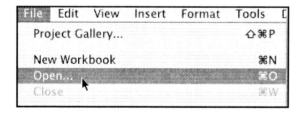 

3. Click your **Gradebook Template** workbook file to select it.
4. Click **OK**.
5. If you are using a Mac, click **File** on the Menu bar.
6. Click **Open**.
7. At the Open dialog window, navigate to the **My Templates** folder.
8. Click the **Gradebook Template** workbook file to select it.
9. Then click **Open**.

Adding Student Names to the Grade Roster Using AutoFill

Use the AutoFill feature to add Student 1 through Student 10 under the Names label—unless you really prefer to type in actual student names.

10. Click in cell **A3** and type the following: Student 1

11. Use the AutoFill feature to enter Student 2 through Student 10 in cells A4 through A12. Using your mouse, point to the fill handle—the small square at the bottom-right corner of the active cell (A3). When the cell pointer is positioned on the fill handle, it changes to a black cross. Click when you see the black cross and drag the fill handle down, highlighting cells **A4 through A12**. Release the mouse button. Student 2 through Student 10 will automatically appear in the highlighted cells.

Adjusting the Column Width

Notice that Column A is not wide enough to display all the text for Student 10. So, make it a bit wider.

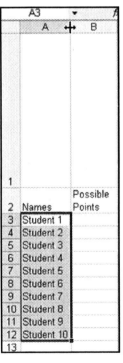

12. Point your cursor to the separator line between column heading A and column heading B.

13. Double-click to automatically widen the column width just enough for Student 10 to display completely.

Entering the Possible Points for Each Assignment

As you enter the possible points for each assignment, watch the Total in cell I2 increase.

14. Click in cell **C2** and type the following: **20**

15. Click in cell **D2** and type the following: **60**

16. Click in cell **E2** and type the following: **25**

17. Click in cell **F2** and type the following: **30**

18. Click in cell **G2** and type the following: **100**

19. Click in cell **H2** when you are finished, allowing *Microsoft Excel* to calculate your last entry.

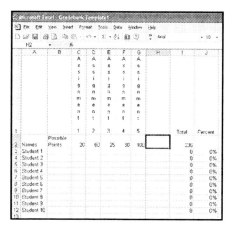 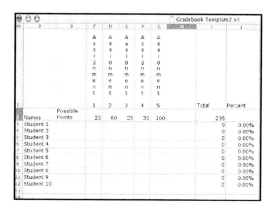

Wow! Did you see how the Total increased with each entry?

Entering Student Scores

20. Now enter student scores that are equal to or less than the Possible Points for each assignment—unless you're giving extra credit!

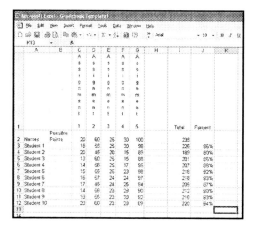 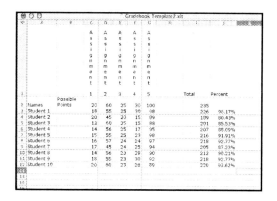

21. Click in cell **K13** when you are finished, allowing *Microsoft Excel* to calculate your last entry.

Changing a Student Grade

One of the beauties of using an electronic gradebook is the ease with which you can change a student's grade without recalculating the final grade. *Microsoft Excel* does it for you automatically.

Imagine that Student 4 came to you with Assignment 5, asking you to reconsider your grading of one of the items. You agree that Student 4's grade should be increased by five points. Click in cell **G6** and type Student 4's new score. (Simply add five points to whatever value you have for Assignment 5 and enter it. The old score will disappear and be replaced by the new score.) Click in cell **A13** when you are finished, allowing *Microsoft Excel* to calculate your last entry. Watch how the Total and Percent values for Student 4 automatically change, reflecting the new score.

Saving the Completed Gradebook

That's it for this gradebook. So save the changes you have made.

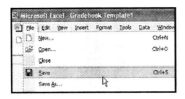   

22. Click **File** on the Menu bar.
23. Click **Save**.

—or—

24. Click the **Save** button on the Standard toolbar.

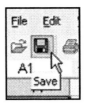   

25. At the **Save As** dialog window, click the Save in list arrow and navigate to where you want to save your gradebook.

26. Click in the **File name** textbox and type the following: **Gradebook for First Nine Weeks**

27. Click OK.

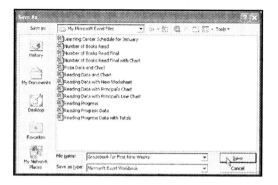 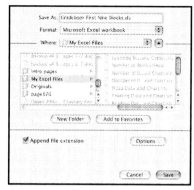

Closing the Workbook and Exiting *Microsoft Excel*

28. To close your workbook, click **File** on the Menu bar.

29. Click **Close**.

—or—

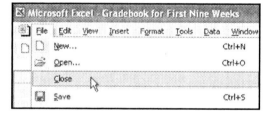 

30. Click the **Close Window** button.

31. Exit *Microsoft Excel*.

Congratulations upon your completion of the **Teacher Activities That Teach**.
Now you are ready for some real fun—using *Microsoft Excel* with your students.

Student Lessons for Learning

If You . . . Book Favorites
Grades K-4

Lesson Summary

In this lesson, students read five books from the Laura Numeroff *If You . . .* series. Then students vote for their favorites. Students enter their votes into a *Microsoft Excel* workbook and chart the results.

Curricular Content

- Reading
- Discussing stories, including comparing and contrasting
- Interpreting column charts

Computer Skills

- Spreadsheet text entry
- Spreadsheet data entry
- Spreadsheet simple formatting
- Charting

Before the Computer

- Gather and display five books written by Laura Numeroff, such as *If You Give a Mouse a Cookie, If Give a Mouse a Muffin, If You Give a Pig a Pancake, If You Take a Mouse to School,* and *If You Take a Mouse to the Movies.*

- Read all five stories either as a class (aloud) or in small groups (to each other).

- Compare and contrast the five stories with students. Discuss the characters, their activities, and more.

- Using a display of hands, have students vote for their favorite *If You . . .* book.

At the Computer

Launch *Microsoft Excel.*

1. Click in cell **A1** and type the following: **Books**
2. Click in cell **B1** and type the following: **Number of Votes**
3. Click on the **row heading 1** to select the entire row.
4. Click the **Bold button** on the **Formatting** toolbar.

 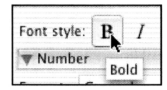

5. Click the **Center button** on the **Formatting** toolbar.

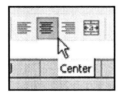 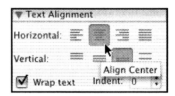

6. Click in cell **A2** and type the name of the first Laura Numeroff book, such as **If You Give a Mouse a Cookie**.
7. Click in cell **A3** and type the name of the second Laura Numeroff book, such as **If You Give a Moose a Muffin**.
8. Click in cell **A4** and type the name of the third Laura Numeroff book, such as **If You Give a Pig a Pancake**.
9. Click in cell **A5** and type the name of the fourth Laura Numeroff book, such as **If You Take a Mouse to School**.
10. Click in cell **A6** and type the name of the fifth Laura Numeroff book, such as **If You Take a Mouse to the Movies**.
11. Resize **column A and column B**, so that all of your contents are displayed properly. (If necessary, see **Teacher Activity 3—Adjusting Column Widths.**)

12. Click in cell **B2** and type the number of students who voted for the first Laura Numeroff book, such as **6**.

13. Click in cell **B3** and type the number of students who voted for the second Laura Numeroff book, such as **7**.

14. Click in cell **B4** and type the number of students who voted for the third Laura Numeroff book, such as **3**.

15. Click in cell **B5** and type the number of students who voted for the fourth Laura Numeroff book, such as **4**.

16. Click in cell **B6** and type the number of students who voted for the fifth Laura Numeroff book, such as **5**.

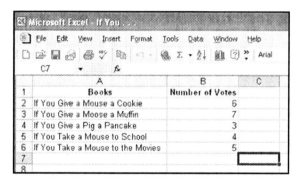

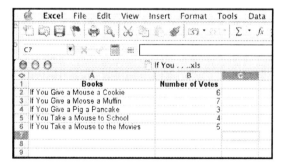

17. Save your work.

18. To create a chart, select (highlight) cells **A1 through B5**.

19. Click the **Chart Wizard** button on the Standard toolbar.

20. At the **Chart Wizard – Step 1 of 4 – Chart Type** dialog box, select the **Chart type**, such as **Column**.

21. Select the **Chart subtype**, such as **Clustered Column**.

22. Click **Next**.

23. At the **Chart Wizard – Step 2 of 4 – Chart Source Data** dialog box, click **Next**.

24. At the **Chart Wizard – Step 3 of 4 – Chart Options** dialog box, click in the **Chart title** textbox and type the following: **Our Favorite Books**

25. Click in the **Category (X)** axis textbox and type the following: **Books**

26. Click in the **Value (Y)** axis textbox and type the following: **Number of Books**

27 Click the **Legend** tab to bring it to the forefront.

28. Click in the **Show legend** box to deselect it. (The legend will disappear from your chart display.)

29. Click **Next**.

30. At the **Chart Wizard—Step 4 of 4—Chart Location** dialog box, click the **As new sheet** button.

31. Click in the **As new sheet** textbox and type the following: **Our Favorite Books**

32. Click **Finish**.

33. The **Our Favorite Books** chart now appears on its own worksheet.

34. Save your work.

35. Print your chart.

36. Exit *Microsoft Excel*.

Assessment

- Have students interpret the chart display. According to the chart, which book was the most favorite? Which book was the least favorite?

Extension

- Have students create their own *If You . . .* stories.

Related CD Files

- **If You . . . .xls** (a copy of the *Microsoft Excel* workbook used in this student lesson)

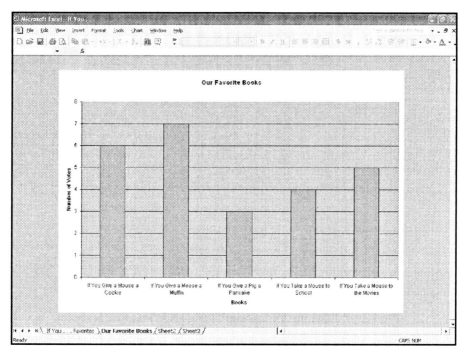

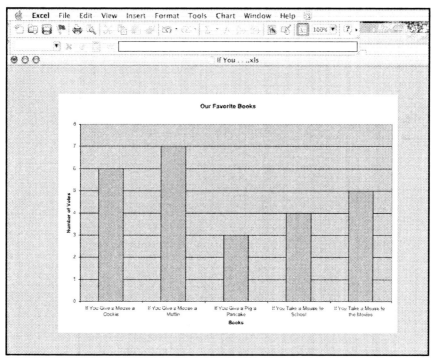

Pets Galore
Grades K-4

Lesson Summary

Most children love animals. Many of your students have pets of their own. But what kinds are they? What are some of the more unusual pets? In this lesson, students collect information from their classmates about the kinds of pets they have. Students enter this information into a *Microsoft Excel* worksheet and create a chart. Optionally, students may also create a pictograph.

Curriculum Content

- Discussing animals and pets
- Collecting survey data
- Using a tally sheet
- Interpreting bar charts and pictographs

Computer Skills

- Spreadsheet text entry
- Spreadsheet data entry
- Spreadsheet simple formatting
- Charting

Materials

- **Pets Galore Data Organizer**
- Books about pets

Before the Computer

- Display the books about pets.
- Select one or two books to read to or with students.

- Discuss the types of pets that students own, as well as other unusual pets they have heard about or seen.

- Explain to students that they will be gathering information about the types of pets they own.

- Demonstrate to students how to use the **Pets Galore Data Organizer**.

- Provide each student with a **Pets Galore Data Organizer**. Direct students to complete their surveys.

- Once the surveys are complete, help students tally their results.

At the Computer

1. Launch *Microsoft Excel*.
2. Click in cell **A1** and type following the column label: **Pets Galore**
3. Click and drag (highlight) from cell A1 through cell G1.
4. Click the **Bold** button on the Formatting toolbar.
5. Click the **Merge and Center** button on the Formatting toolbar.
6. Click the **Font Size** list arrow on the Formatting toolbar.
7. Select **12** points.
8. Click in cell **B2** and type the following column label: **Dogs**
9. Click in cell **C2** and type the following column label: **Cats**
10. Click in cell **D2** and type the following column label: **Birds**
11. Click in cell **E2** and type the following column label: **Fish**
12. Click in cell **F2** and type the following column label: **Hamsters**
13. Click in cell **G2** and type the following column label: **Turtles**

Note: Feel free to add to or change the column labels to align with the pets your students have.

14. Click on the **row heading 1** to select the entire row.
15. Click the **Bold** button on the Formatting toolbar.
16. Click the **Center** button on the Formatting toolbar.
17. Click in cell **A3** and type the following row label: **Boys**
18. Click in cell **A4** and type the following row label: **Girls**
19. Click in cell **A5** and type the following row label: **Total**
20. Click on the **column heading A** to select the entire row.
21. Click the **Bold** button on the Formatting toolbar twice.
22. Enter the survey data in cells **A3 through G4**.
23. Click in cell **B5**.
24. Click the **AutoSum** button on the Standard toolbar.
25. Click the **Enter** button to the left of the Formula bar.

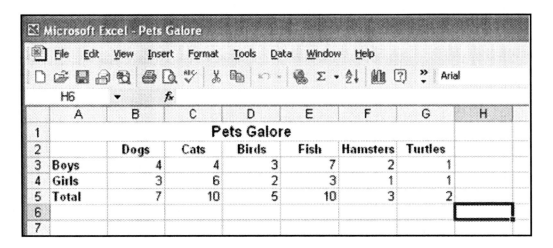

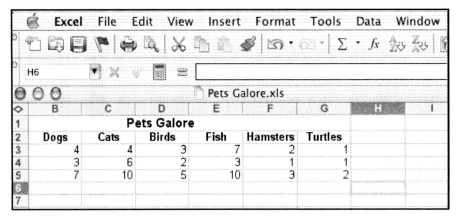

26. Using the **AutoFill** feature, click and drag the fill handle from cell **B5** to cell **G5**.

27. Save your work.

28. To create a chart, select (highlight) cells **A2 through G5**.

29. Click the **Chart Wizard** button on the Standard toolbar.

30. At the **Chart Wizard – Step 1 of 4 – Chart Type** dialog box, select the **Chart type**, such as **Bar**.

31. Select the **Chart subtype**, such as **Clustered Bar**.

32. Click **Next**.

33. At the **Chart Wizard – Step 2 of 4 – Chart Source Data** dialog box, click **Next**.

34. At the **Chart Wizard – Step 3 of 4 – Chart Options** dialog box, click in the **Chart title** textbox and type the following: **Pets Galore**

35. Click in the **Category (X)** axis textbox and type the following: **Our Pets**

36. Click in the **Value (Y) axis** textbox and type the following: **Number of Pets**

37. Click **Next**.

38. At the **Chart Wizard – Step 4 of 4 Chart Location** dialog box, click the **As new sheet** button.

39. Click in the **As new sheet** textbox and type the following: **Pets Galore**

40. Click **Finish**.

41. The **Pets Galore** chart now appears on its own worksheet.

42. Save your work.

43. Print your chart.

44. Exit *Microsoft Excel* or continue with the following optional instructions for converting the bar chart to a pictograph.

Converting the Bar Chart to a Pictograph (Optional)

Materials

- Digital pictures or graphics of pets

Before the Computer

- Find a digital graphic or picture of each type of pet listed in your **Pets Galore** worksheet and chart.

- Save each digital file in a **Pets Galore** folder on your computer system (to assure easy access).

At the Computer

1. To create a pictograph, display your **Pets Galore** worksheet.

2. Click the **row heading 2** to select (highlight) the entire row.

3. Hold down the Control key on your keyboard and click the **row heading 5** (the **Total** row) to select (highlight) the entire row.

4. (Click the **Chart Wizard** button on the Standard toolbar.

5. At the **Chart Wizard – Step 1 of 4 – Chart Type** dialog box, select the **Chart type**, such as **Column**.

6. Select the **Chart subtype**, such as **Clustered Column**.

7. Click **Next**.

8. At the **Chart Wizard – Step 2 of 4 – Chart Source Data** dialog box, click **Next**.

9. At the **Chart Wizard – Step 3 of 4 – Chart Options** dialog box, click in the **Chart title** textbox and type the following: **Pets Pictograph**

10. Click in the **Category (X)** axis textbox and type the following: **Our Pets**

11. Click in the **Value (Y)** axis textbox and type the following: **Number of Pets**

12. Click the Legend tab to bring it to the forefront.

13. Click **Show Legend** to deselect it and remove the legend from the display.

14. Click **Next**.

15. At the **Chart Wizard – Step 4 of 4 Chart Location** dialog box, click the **As new sheet** button.

16. Click in the **As new sheet** textbox and type the following: **Pets Pictograph**

17. Click **Finish**.

18. The **Pets Galore** chart now appears on its own worksheet.

19. Save your work.

20. To change your bar chart to a pictograph, single click on the first bar that represents the first pet, such as **Dogs**. (Notice that this selects the entire series.)

21. Single click on the first bar again. (Notice that this selects only this bar.)

22. Double-click on the bar.

23. At the **Format Data Point** dialog box, click the **Patterns** tab to bring it to the forefront, if it is not already there.

24. Click the **Fill Effects** button.

25. At the **Fill Effects** dialog box, click the **Picture** tab to bring it to the forefront.

26. Click the **Select Picture** button.

27. At the **Select Picture** dialog box, navigate to the folder where you saved your digital graphics or pictures representing the pets.

28. Select the file representing the pet for this bar, such as the **dog**.

29. Click **Insert**.

30. At the **Fill Effects** dialog box, click **Stack and scale to** under Format.

31. In the **Units/Pictures** textbox, type the following: **1**

32. Click **OK**.

33. At the **Format Data Point** dialog box, click **OK**.

34. The graphic or picture of the represented pet now appears within the column.

35. Continue in this manner with each pet column.

36. Save your work

37. Print your pictograph.

Assessment

- Using the **Pets Galore** chart and the **Pets Pictographs** as a reference, have students interpret the information displayed.

Extension

- Have students illustrate how they take care of their pets.

- Have students write and/or illustrate simple stories about their own pets. For students who do not own pets, allow them to write about imaginary pets.

Related CD Files

- **Pets Galore.xls** (a copy of the **Pets Galore** workbook used in this student lesson)

- **Pets Galore Data Organizer.doc** (a copy of the **Pets Galore Data Organizer** referred to in this student lesson—a *Microsoft Word* file)

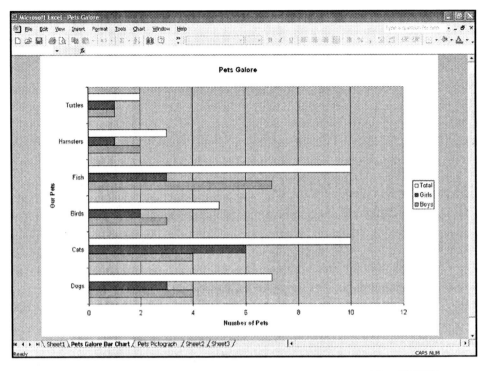

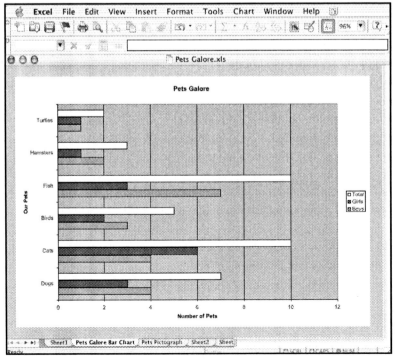

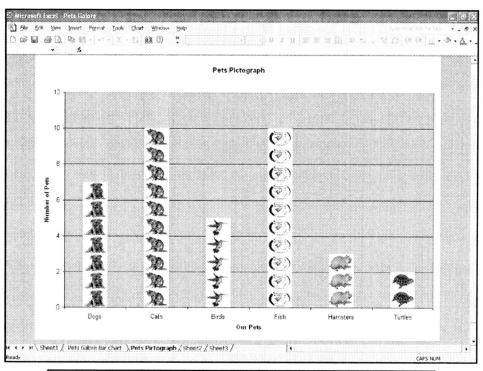

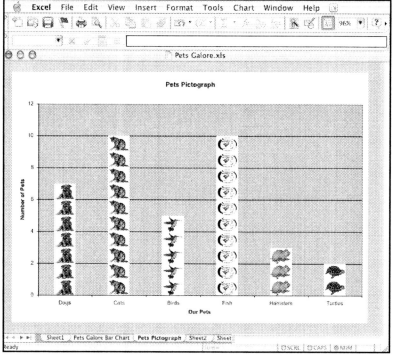

Pets Galore Data Organizer

	Dogs	Cats	Birds	Hamsters	Turtles	Snakes
Boys						
Girls						

Pets Galore Data Organizer

	Dogs	Cats	Birds	Hamsters	Turtles	Snakes
Boys						
Girls						

Author Awards—Rating Story Elements
Grades 3-8

Lesson Summary

In this lesson, students select five authors, analyze their books, and rate their story elements, such as the characters, plot, setting, conflict, and theme, using a *Microsoft Excel* workbook.

Students select five authors from a teacher-developed list. Then students select one book written by each author to read and analyze. Students compare the authors' works and rate each author's book—on a scale of 1 to 5—for his or her development and presentation of characters, plot, setting, conflict, and theme.

Students enter their ratings into a *Microsoft Excel* workbook and average each author's ratings. Students also generate a chart and determine which authors deserve Author Awards.

Curricular Content

- Reading literature
- Analyzing story elements (characters, plot, setting, conflict, and theme)
- Comparing story elements among authors
- Rating story elements

Computer Skills

- Spreadsheet text entry

Author Awards—Rating Story Elements

- Spreadsheet data entry
- Spreadsheet simple formatting
- Spreadsheet simple formulas (average)
- Charting

Before the Computer

- Have students select five authors from a teacher-developed list.
- Have students select one book written by each of the five authors.
- Have students read the books.
- Have students analyze and discuss each author's development and presentation of characters, plot, setting, conflict, and theme.
- Have students rank the authors in each of the five story element categories as follows:
    - The best author in each story element category receives a 5.
    - The second best author in each story element category receives a 4.
    - The third best author in each story element category receives a 3.
    - The fourth best author in each story element category receives a 2.
    - The fifth best author in each story element category receives a 1.

At the Computer

1. Launch *Microsoft Excel.*
2. Click in cell **A1** and type the following column label: **Story Elements**
3. Adjust the width of column **A**.
4. Click in cell **B1** and type the last name of the first author or **Author 1**.
5. Click in cell **C1** and type the last name of the second author or **Author 2**.

6. Click in cell **D1** and type the last name of the third author or **Author 3**.

7. Click in cell **E1** and type the last name of the fourth author or **Author 4**.

8. Click in cell **F1** and type the last name of the fifth author or **Author 5**.

9. Click on the **row heading 1** to select (highlight) the entire row.

10. Click the **Bold** button on the Formatting toolbar.

11. Click the **Center** button on the Formatting toolbar.

12. Click in cell **A2** and type the following row label: **Characters**

13. Click in cell **A3** and type the following row label: **Plot**

14. Click in cell **A4** and type the following row label: **Setting**

15. Click in cell **A5** and type the following row label: **Conflict**

16. Click in cell **A6** and type the following row label: **Theme**

17. Click in cell **A7** and type the following row label: **Average**

18. Click on **column heading A** to select (highlight) the entire column.

19. Click the **Bold** button on the Formatting toolbar **twice**.

20. Enter the author rankings for the story elements in cells **B2 through F6**.

21. Click in cell **B7**, where the average for Author 1 will be displayed.

22. Click **Insert** on the Menu bar.

23. Click **Function**.

24. At the **Insert Function** dialog box, select **AVERAGE** under **Select a function**.

25. Click **OK**.

26. Using the **AutoFill** feature, click and drag the fill handle from cell **B7** to cell **F7**.

27. Click on the **row heading 7** to select (highlight) the entire row.

28. Click the **Bold** button on the Formatting toolbar twice.

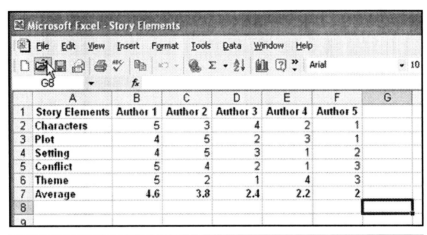

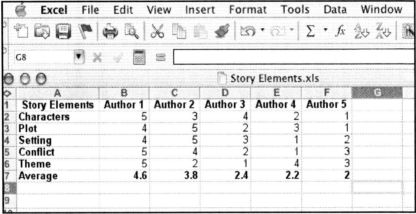

29. Save your work.

30. To create a chart, click on **row heading 1** to select (highlight) the entire row.

31. Hold down the **Control key** on your keyboard and click on **row heading 7** to select the entire row for charting as well.

32. Click the **Chart Wizard** button on the Standard toolbar.

33. At the **Chart Wizard – Step 1 of 4 – Chart Type** dialog box, select **Column**.

34. Select the **Chart subtype**, such as **Clustered column with a 3-D visual effect**.

35. Click **Next**.

36. At the **Chart Wizard – Step 2 of 4 – Chart Source Data** dialog box, click **Next**.

37. At the **Chart Wizard – Step 3 of 4 – Chart Options** dialog box, click on the **Titles** tab to bring it to the forefront, if it is not already there.
38. Click in the **Chart title** textbox and type the following: **Author Awards**
39. Click in the **Category (X) axis** textbox and type the following: **Authors**
40. Click in the **Category (Y) axis** textbox and type the following: **Average Rating**
41. Click the **Legend** tab to bring it to the forefront.
42. Click in the **Show legend** box to deselect it. (The legend will disappear from your chart display.)
43. Click **Next**.
44. At the **Chart Wizard – Step 4 of 4 – Chart Location** window, click the **As new sheet** button.
45. Click in the **As new sheet** textbox and type the following: **Author Awards**
46. Click **Finish**.
47. The **Author Awards** chart now appears on its own worksheet.
48. Save your work.
49. Print your chart.
50. Exit *Microsoft Excel*.

Assessment

- Using the Author Awards chart as a reference, have students interpret the information displayed.

Extension

- Have students chart the Author Awards by story element.
- Have students create Author Awards certificates in *Microsoft PowerPoint* for the best author in each story element category.

Related CD Files

- **Author Awards.xls** (a copy of the Author Awards workbook used in this student lesson)

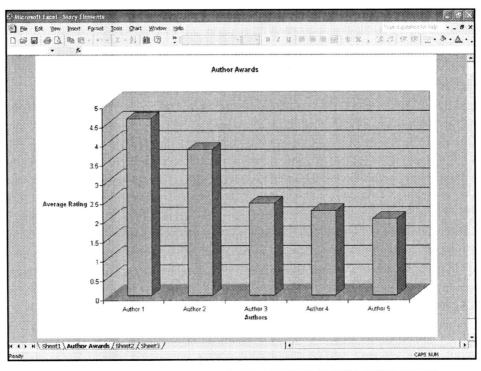

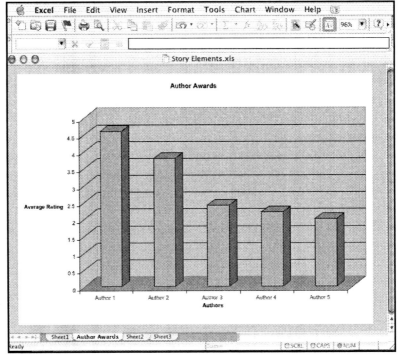

Actors and Animals
Grades 3-8

Lesson Summary

In this lesson, actors, actresses, and animal stories come together. Students read classic animal stories and decide which actors and actresses would be best to provide the voices for the animal parts in an animated movie.

Curriculum Content

- Reading classic animal stories
- Researching actors and actresses
- Conducting a survey
- Tallying survey data
- Using oral language skills—persuasion

Computer Skills

- Spreadsheet text entry
- Spreadsheet data entry
- Spreadsheet simple formatting
- Charting

Materials

- **Actors and Animals Voting Tally Sheet**

Before the Computer

- If possible, show an animal movie such as **Charlotte's Web** or **Babe** and discuss how the "human" voices fit the animal characters.
- Have students read different classic animal stories and choose one that can be used as the foundation for an animated movie.

- Brainstorm a list of actors and actresses that might be the "voices" in the book students choose to make into a movie.
- Have students form small groups (three or four students each). Let each group select five or six characters from the book and five or six actors and actresses that could voice the animal parts.
- Have each group survey 50 people and record their votes on the **Actors and Animals Voting Tally Sheet**.

At the Computer

1. Launch *Microsoft Excel*.
2. Before entering column labels, format the first row for wrapped text. Click on **row heading 1** to select (highlight) the entire row.
3. Click **Format** on the Menu bar.
4. Click **Cells**.
5. At the **Format Cells** dialog box, click on the **Alignment** tab to bring it to the forefront.
6. Click **Wrap text** under **Text control**.
7. Click **OK**.

Note: In this sample spreadsheet, the characters from Rudyard Kipling's *The Jungle Book* are being used.

8. Click in cell **A1** and type the following: **Characters**
9. Click in cell **B1** and type the name of the first actor or actress, such as **Tom Cruise**.

Note: Notice that as you type in an actor or actresses name that exceeds the width of the column, the text automatically wraps, creating a second line.

10. Click in cell **C1** and type the name of the second actor or actress, such as **Kevin Costner**.
11. Click in cell **D1** and type the name of the third actor or actress, such as **Robin Williams**.
12. Click in cell **E1** and type the name of the fourth actor or actress, such as **Eddie Murphy**.
13. Click in cell **F1** and type the name of the fifth actor or actress, such as **Julia Roberts**.
14. Click in cell **G1** and type the name of the sixth actor or actress, such as **Demi Moore**.

15. Continue in this manner until all the actors and actresses you selected for possible animal voice parts are entered into your worksheet.

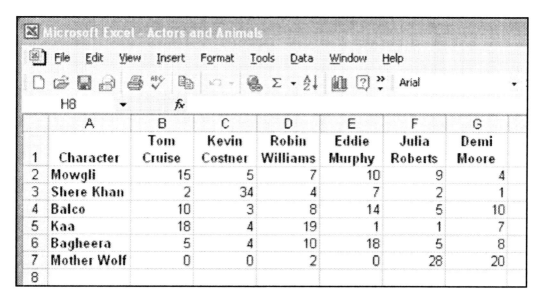

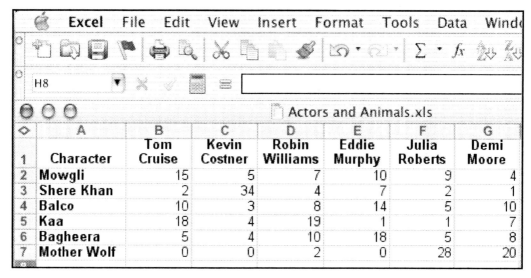

16. Click on the **row heading 1** to select the entire row.
17. Click the **Bold** button on the Formatting toolbar.

18. Click the **Center** button on the Formatting toolbar.
19. Adjust the width of **column A**, if necessary.
20. Click in cell **A2** and type the name of the first animal character, such a **Mowgli**.
21. Click in cell **A3** and type the name of the second animal character, such as **Shere Khan**.
22. Click in cell **A4** and type the name of the third animal character, such as **Baloo**.
23. Click in cell **A5** and type the name of the fourth animal character, such as **Ka**.
24. Click in cell **A6** and type the name of the fifth animal character, such as **Bagheera**.
25. Click in cell **A7** and type the name of the sixth animal character, such as **Mother Wolf**.
26. Continue in this manner until all the animal characters you selected are entered into your worksheet.
27. Click on the **column heading A** to select the entire column.
28. Click the **Bold** button on the Formatting toolbar twice.
29. Adjust the width of **column A**, if necessary.
30. Enter the survey data in cells **B2 through G7** (or whatever range of cells corresponds with your actors, actresses, and animal character entries).
31. Save your work.
32. To see which actor or actress received the largest percentage of votes for your first character, click the **row heading 1** to select the entire row for charting.
33. Hold down the **Control key** on your keyboard.
34. Click the **row heading 2** to select the entire row for charting.
35. Click the **Chart Wizard** button on the Standard toolbar.
36. At the **Chart Wizard – Step 1 of 4 – Chart Type** dialog box, select the **Chart type**, such as **Pie**.
37. Select the **Chart subtype**, such as **Exploded pie with a 3-D visual effect chart**.
38. Click **Next**.
39. At the **Chart Wizard – Step 2 of 4 – Chart Source Data** dialog box, click **Next**.

40. At the **Chart Wizard – Step 3 of 4 – Chart Options** dialog box, click in the **Chart title** textbox and type the following: **Who Should Play Mowgli?** (Of course, you should substitute the name of your character for Mowgli.)
41. Click the **Legend** tab to bring it to the forefront.
42. Click the **Show legend** box to deselect it. (The legend will disappear from your chart display.)
43. Click the **Data Labels** tab to bring it to the forefront.
44. Under **Label Contains**, click **Category name**.
45. Under **Label Contains**, click **Percentage**.
46. Click **Next**.
47. At the **Chart Wizard – Step 4 of 4 – Chart Location** dialog box, click the **As new sheet** button.
48. Click in the **As new sheet** textbox and type the following: **Actors and Animals 1**.
49. Click **Finish**.
50. The **Actors and Animals 1** chart now appears on its own worksheet.
51. Save your work.
52. Print your chart.
53. Return to **Sheet1** and continue generating the same type of chart for each remaining character.
54. When you are finished, exit *Microsoft Excel*.

Assessment

- Have each group of students present and discuss the survey findings to the class, using charts for visual displays.

Extension

- Have each group of students create a different type of chart, such as a bar chart or a column chart, to display their findings in another way.

Related CD Files

- **Actors and Animals.xls** (a copy of the **Actors and Animals** workbook used in this student lesson)
- **Actors and Animals Voting Tally Sheet.doc** (a copy of the **Actors and Animals Voting Tally Sheet** referred to in this student lesson—a *Microsoft Word* file)

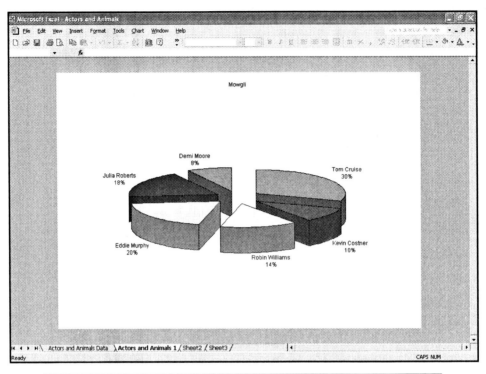

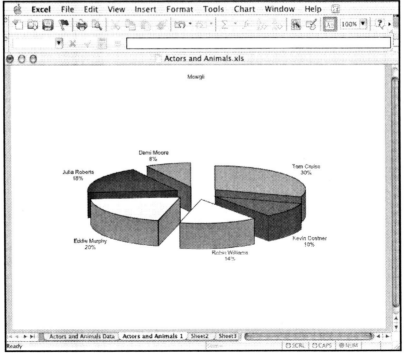

Actors and Animals Voting Tally Sheet

Actors→ Characters↓									

Directions: Fill in the names of the actors and actresses in the top row of cells. Fill in the names of the characters in the first column of cells. As you conduct your survey, enter a tally mark for the actor or actress each person selects to play each character.

Actors and Animals Voting Tally Sheet

Actors→ Characters↓									

Directions: Fill in the names of the actors and actresses in the top row of cells. Fill in the names of the characters in the first column of cells. As you conduct your survey, enter a tally mark for the actor or actress each person selects to play each character.

Guess and Test
Grades 1–5

Lesson Summary

In this lesson, students guess (estimate) and then test (count) how many colored objects (candies, cereal, beads, etc.) are in their cups. First they record their estimates in a *Microsoft Excel* worksheet. Then they test (count) and record the actual amount in the worksheet as well. Students create a clustered column (double bar) chart to compare their guess and test or estimated and actual number of colored objects.

Curriculum Content

- Naming colors
- Estimating
- Sorting and grouping objects into sets
- Counting
- Charting

Computer Skills

- Spreadsheet text entry
- Spreadsheet data entry
- Spreadsheet simple formatting
- Charting

Materials

- Colored objects (five or six colors), such as candies (M & Ms), cereal (Fruit Loops), or small beads sufficient enough to allow one small cup (holding 1-2 ounces) per student
- Small opaque plastic cups (2-3 ounce Solo cups) sufficient enough to allow one per student and one for you

Before the Computer

- Fill the opaque plastic cups half full of the colored objects. Before passing out the cups, announce cup-handling rules that may include:
  - No stirring of the colored objects.
  - No shaking of the colored objects.
  - If candies or cereal are used, no eating of the colored objects until you are told it is time to do so.
  - Partial or broken candies, cereal pieces, or beads do not count.

At the Computer

1. Launch *Microsoft Excel*.
2. Without stirring or shaking (just peering over their cups), elicit from students the colors of the objects they see.
3. Click in cell **B1** and type the name of the first color that students see, such as **Red**.
4. Click in cell **C1** and type the name of the second color that students see, such as **Green**.
5. Click in cell **D1** and type the name of the third color that students see, such as **Yellow**.
6. Click in cell **E1** and type the name of the fourth color that students see, such as **Orange**.
7. Click in cell **F1** and type the name of the fifth color that students see, such as **Brown**.
8. Click in cell **G1** and type the name of the sixth color that students see, such as **Blue**.
9. Click on the **row heading 1** to select (highlight) the entire row.
10. Click the **Bold** button on the Formatting toolbar.
11. Click the **Center** button on the Formatting toolbar.
12. Click in cell **A2** and type the following: **Guess**
13. Without stirring or shaking, have students estimate the number of colored objects they have in their cups.
14. Enter selected guesses for each color listed in cells **B2, C2, D2, E2, F2, and G2**.

15. Have students pour out their cups of objects and separate them into sets based upon their colors.

16. Have students count the number of colored objects they have for each set of colors.

17. Click in cell **A3** and type the following: **Test**

18. Click on the **column heading A** to select (highlight) it.

19. Click the **Bold** button on the Formatting toolbar twice.

20. Enter selected actual numbers of colored objects for each color listed in cells **B3, C3, D3, E3, F3, and G3**.

21. Save your work.

22. To create a chart, select (highlight) cells **A1 through G3**.

23. Click the **Chart Wizard** button on the Standard toolbar.

24. At the **Chart Wizard – Step 1 or 4 – Chart Type** window, click on the Standard Types tab to bring it to the forefront, if necessary.

25. At the **Chart type** menu, select **Column**.

26. At the **Chart sub-type** menu, select the **Clustered column**—the first on in the first row.

27. Click **Next**.

28. At the **Chart Wizard – Step 2 of 4 – Chart Source Data** window, click **Next**.

29. At the **Chart Wizard – Step 3 of 4 – Chart Options** window, click on the **Titles** tab to bring it to the forefront, if necessary.

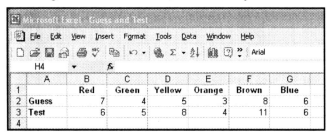

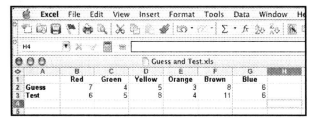

30. Click in the **Chart title** textbox and type the following: **Guess and Test**
31. In the **Category (X)** axis, type the following: **Colors**
32. In the **Value (Y)** axis, type the following: **Numbers**
33. Click **Next**.
34. At the **Chart Wizard – Step 4 of 4 – Chart Location** window, click the **As new sheet** button.
35. Click in the **As new sheet** textbox and type the following: **Guess and Test**
36. Click **Finish**.
37. The **Guess and Test** chart should now appear on its own worksheet.
38. Save your work.
39. Print your chart.
40. Exit *Microsoft Excel*.
41. If you provided candy or cereal, allow students to eat their colored objects.

Assessment

- Print the chart to share with your students. Discuss the estimated versus the actual number of colored objects for each color. Question students about their data. For example, you may ask, "How many of you were able to guess the number of objects correctly for one (two or three) colors?" or "Who had more red objects than they estimated?" Use terms appropriate for their mathematical abilities when comparing findings, including more than, greater than, fewer than, less than, equal to, the same as, etc. Have students verbalize the relationships between their estimated and actual number of colored objects.

Extension

- Discuss the color words listed on the chart. Use the color words to integrate several related language arts concepts. For example, have students spell the color words aloud; identify objects in the classroom with the same colors; think of other words with the same initial consonant sounds, medial vowel sounds, etc.; offer words that rhyme with the color words; discuss the homophones red/read and blue/blew or the homonyms orange and yellow.

Supporting Resources

- If you used M & M candies, visit the M & M web site on the Internet at **www.m-ms.com** for supporting materials.
- If available, provide your students with *The M & Ms Counting Book* by Barbara Barbieri McGrath (ISBN 0-88106-853-5).

Related CD Files

- **Guess and Test.xls** (a copy of the **Guess and Test** workbook file used in this student lesson)

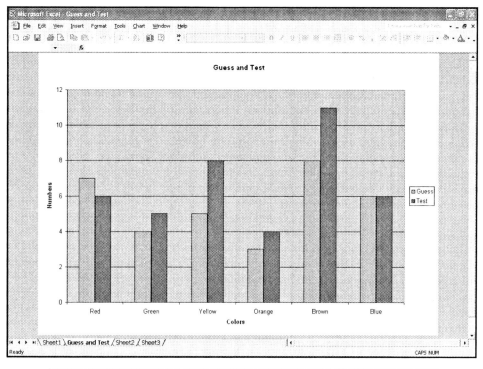

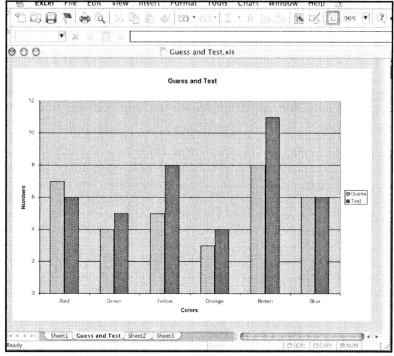

Best Meal Deal
Grades 4 and Up

Lesson Summary

In this lesson, students gather data about the prices of fast foods at local restaurants. They enter their data into a *Microsoft Excel* worksheet to calculate the best meal deal.

Curriculum Concepts

- Comparing prices

Computer Skills

- Spreadsheet text entry
- Spreadsheet data entry
- Spreadsheet simple formatting
- Spreadsheet simple formulas (sum)
- Charting

Materials

- **Best Meal Deal Data Organizer**

Before the Computer

- After reading through this activity, determine whether you would like it completed by individual, paired, or small groups of students.
- First, introduce students to the task of gathering food-pricing information from local fast-food restaurants. (If for some reason students are unable to gather such data, provide them with menus or handouts of fast food prices.)
- Discuss and agree upon standard weights and sizes for comparing hamburgers, French fries, and milkshakes. For example, students will gather prices of quarter-pound hamburgers, large French fries, and medium-size milkshakes.
- Provide students with copies of the **Best Meal Deal Student Data Organizer**. Review the directions.

- Discuss with students the basic components of a worksheet, navigation techniques, and the types of data input (text, numbers, and formulas). Demonstrate to students how data is entered; how columns and rows are selected, formatted, and resized; and how formulas are used to add up and average food prices.
- Model the creation of a Best Meal Deal worksheet. Enter the names of two local fast food restaurants and possible prices for hamburgers, French fries, and milkshakes.

At the Computer

1. Launch *Microsoft Excel*.
2. Click in cell **A1** and type the following: **Restaurant**
3. Click in cell **B1** and type the following: **Hamburger**
4. Click in cell **C1** and type the following: **French Fries**
5. Click in cell **D1** and type the following: **Milkshake**
6. Click in cell **E1** and type the following: **Total**
7. Click on **row heading 1** to select (highlight) the entire row.
8. Click the **Bold** button on the Formatting toolbar.
9. While row 1 is still selected, adjust the column widths. Click **Format** on the Menu bar.
10. Click **Column**.
11. Click **AutoFit Selection**.
12. Click in cell **A2** and enter the name of the first fast-food restaurant, such as **Wendy's**
13. Click in cell **A3** and enter the name of the second fast-food restaurant, such as **McDonald's**
14. Click in cell **A4** and enter the name of the third fast-food restaurant, such as **Burger King**
15. Continue in this manner until all the restaurants are entered into your worksheet.
16. Click the **column heading A** to select (highlight) the entire column.
17. Hold down the Control key on your keyboard and click the **column heading E** to select (highlight) the entire column as well.
18. Click the **Bold** button on Formatting toolbar **twice**.
19. While the columns are still selected, adjust the column widths. Click **Format** on the Menu bar.

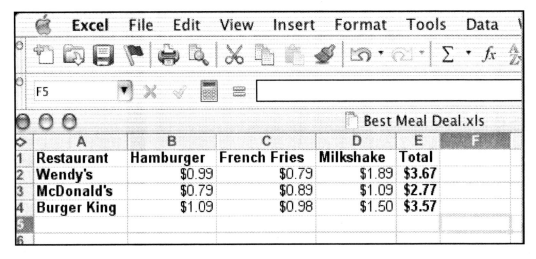

20. Click **Column**.

21. Click **AutoFit Selection**.

22. Select (highlight) cells **B2 through E4** (or the last cell where the **Total** column and last restaurant row intersect).

23. Click **Format** on the Menu bar.

24. Click **Cells**.

25. At the Format Cells dialog box, click the **Number** tab to bring it to the forefront, if necessary.

26. Click **Currency**.

27. Then click **OK**. (Now the cells are formatted for currency with the dollar sign and two numbers displayed after the decimal point.)

28. Click in cell **B2** and enter the cost of a hamburger at the first restaurant.

29. Click in cell **C2** and enter the cost of French fries at the first restaurant.

30. Click in cell **D2** and enter the cost of a milkshake at the first restaurant.

31. Continue in this manner until the cost information for all of the restaurants is entered into your worksheet.

32. Click in cell **E2** and use the AutoSum feature to add up the costs of a hamburger, French fries, and a milkshake at the first restaurant.

Note: AutoSum automatically selects the range of cells from B2 through D2.

33. Click on the **Enter** button to the left of the formula bar to accept this range.

34. Using the **AutoFill** feature, click and drag the fill handle from cell **E2** through **E4** (or to the row for the last restaurant).

35. Save your work.

36. To create a chart, select (highlight) cells **A1 through D4** (or to the last milkshake value in your worksheet).

Note: Do not include the Total column.

37. Click the **Chart Wizard** button on the Standard toolbar.

38. At the **Chart Wizard – Step 1 of 4 – Chart Type** dialog box, select the **Chart type**, such as **Column**.

39. Select the **Chart sub-type**, such as **Stacked Column**.

40. Click **Next**.

41. At the **Chart Wizard – Step 2 of 4 – Chart Source Data** window, click the **Data Range** tab to bring it to the forefront, if necessary.

42. Under Series in, click **Columns**.

43. Then click **Next**.

44. At the **Chart Wizard – Step 3 of 4 – Chart Options** window, click on the **Titles** tab to bring it to the forefront, if it is not already there.

45. Click in the **Chart title** textbox and type the following: **Best Meal Deal**

46. Click in the **Category (X)** axis textbox and type the following: **Restaurants**

47. Click in the **Value (Y)** axis textbox and type the following: **Cost of Meals**

48. Click **Next**.

49. At the **Chart Wizard – Step 4 of 4 – Chart Location** dialog box, click **As new sheet**.

50. Click in the **As new sheet** textbox and type the following: **Best Meal Deal**

51. Click **Finish**.

52. The **Best Meal Deal** chart now appears on its own worksheet.

53. Save your work.

54. Print your chart.

55. Exit *Microsoft Excel.*

Assessment

- Using the **Best Meal Deal** chart as a reference, have students interpret the information provided.

Extension

- Discuss how worksheets can be used to answer "What if . . . ?" questions. Help students experiment with "What if . . . ?" calculations using the **Best Meal Deal** worksheet. For example, what if the first restaurant changes the price of its milkshake to $1.89? Enter this value in the worksheet and see how the new price effects the Total column.

- Using the **Best Meal Deal** worksheet, have student calculate the average cost of eating out at the restaurants listed.

Related CD Files

- **Best Meal Deal.xls** (a copy of the **Best Meal Deal** workbook used in this student lesson)

- **Best Meal Deal Data Organizer.doc** (a copy of the **Best Meal Deal Data Organizer** referred to in this student lesson—a *Microsoft Word* file)

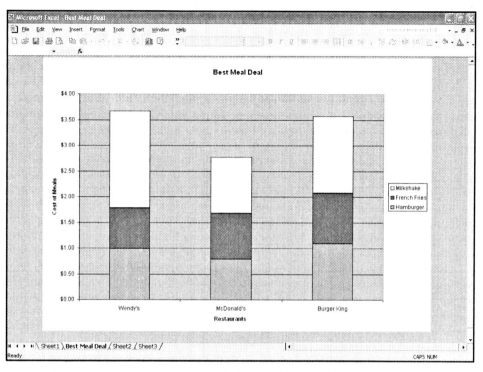

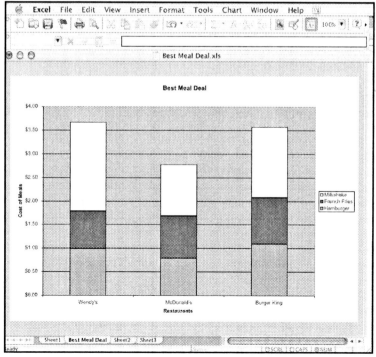

Best Meal Deal
Student Data Organizer

Directions: Visit or call three or four fast-food restaurants in your area. In the table below, record the name of each restaurant and the price of a hamburger, French fries, and a milkshake. Remember to record equivalent amounts of food items. (For example, a quarter-pound hamburger, large French fries, and a medium-sized milkshake.)

Name of Restaurant	Price of Hamburger	Price of French Fries	Price of Milkshake

Best Meal Deal
Student Data Organizer

Directions: Visit or call three or four fast-food restaurants in your area. In the table below, record the name of each restaurant and the price of a hamburger, French fries, and a milkshake. Remember to record equivalent amounts of food items. (For example, a quarter-pound hamburger, large French fries, and a medium-sized milkshake.)

Name of Restaurant	Price of Hamburger	Price of French Fries	Price of Milkshake

Puppy Play Area
Grades 4-6

Lesson Summary

In this lesson, students find the best price for fencing in a play area for their new puppy. Students determine the perimeter of the puppy play area. They collect fence pricing information and record the cost data for different types of fencing from several stores in a *Microsoft Excel* worksheet. Students use a simple formula to calculate the fencing costs. Based upon their findings, students determine which fencing they would purchase for the puppy play area.

Curriculum Concepts

- Gathering data
- Measuring perimeters
- Interpreting information

Computer Skills

- Spreadsheet text entry
- Spreadsheet data entry
- Spreadsheet simple formatting
- Spreadsheet simple formulas
- Charting

Materials

- Graph paper
- **Sample Puppy Play Area Data Organizer**
- **Puppy Play Area Data Organizer**

Before the Computer

- Divide students into small groups of puppy play area teams.
- Have each team of students draw or find a picture that represents its puppy.
- Have each team of students name its puppy.
- Provide each team with graph paper.
- Have each team designate a potential puppy play area at one group member's back yard (or other designated area).
- Have each team determine a scale and plot the measurements representing the puppy play area on graph paper.
- Work with the teams or class as a whole, reviewing how to determine the perimeters of the proposed puppy play areas.
- Have each team present their proposed puppy play area to the class, including an explanation of how the perimeter was determined.
- Share with students the **Sample Puppy Play Area Data Organizer**.
- Have students collect ads from local lumberyards and home improvement stores that list the costs of fencing materials.
- Have students complete the **Puppy Play Area Data Organizer**, using at least three different providers and three different types of fencing.

At the Computer

1. Launch *Microsoft Excel*.
2. Based upon the information recorded in the **Puppy Play Area Data Organizer**, have each team of students create a worksheet that compiles information and calculates the actual fencing costs. (If you prefer, you can create a class puppy play area worksheet, eliciting information from the groups.)
3. Click in cell **A1** and type the following column label: **Type of Fencing**
4. Click in cell **B1** and type the following column label: **Price Per Foot**
5. Click in cell **C1** and type the following column label: **Perimeter in Feet**

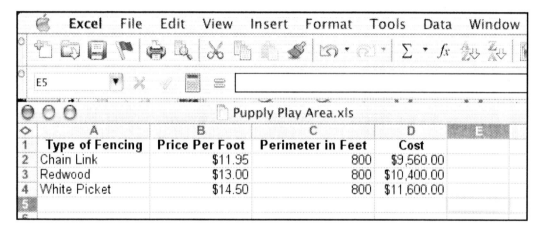

6. Click in cell **D1** and type the following column label: **Cost**

7. Click in cell **A2** and type the first kind of fencing, such as **Chain Link**.

8. Click in cell **A3** and type the second kind of fencing, such as **Redwood**.

9. Click in cell **A4** and type the third kind of fencing, such as **White Picket**.

10. If you have more kinds of fencing, continue typing them in **column A** of the worksheet.

11. Click the **row heading 1** to select (highlight) the entire row.

12. Click the **Bold** button on the Formatting toolbar.

Sample Puppy Play Area Data Organizer

	Lumberyards or Home Improvement Stores			
Types of Fencing ▼	Home Base	Home Depot	Victor's Lumberyard	**Cost Per Foot** ◀
Chain Link	$12.50	$11.95	$13.00	
Redwood	$13.00	$13.49	$15.75	
White Picket	$14.50	$15.50	$12.50	

13. Click the **Center** button on the Formatting toolbar.
14. While the row is still selected, adjust the column widths to accommodate the length of the text displayed. Click **Format** on the Menu bar.
15. Click **Column**.
16. Click **AutoFit Selection**.
17. Click the **column heading A** to select (highlight) the entire row.
18. Click the **Bold** button on the Formatting toolbar twice.
19. To format columns B and D for currency, click the **column heading B** to select (highlight) the entire column.
20. Hold down the **Control key** on your keyboard and click the **column heading D** to select (highlight) the entire column as well.
21. Click **Format** on the Menu bar.

22. Click **Cells**.
23. At the Format Cells dialog box, click the **Number** tab to bring it to the forefront, if necessary.
24. Under **Category**, click **Currency**.
25. Click **OK**.
26. Using information recorded in the **Puppy Play Area Data Organizer**, type the price for the first kind of fencing in cell **B2**. Type only the numeric value, along with the decimal point. *Microsoft Excel* will automatically add the dollar sign and right align the data.
27. Type the price for the second kind of fencing in cell **B3**.
28. Type the price for the third kind of fencing in cell **B4**.
29. Continue typing in the prices for the remaining kinds of fences in column **B**.
30. Click in cell **C2** and type the perimeter of the puppy play area. Enter the numeric value only, rounded to the nearest foot.
31. Use the **AutoFill** feature to enter the same perimeter values in cells **C3 through C4** (or further if you have more kinds of fencing listed).
32. Click in cell **D2** and type the following formula: **=B2*C2**
33. Click the **Enter** button to the left of the formula bar.
34. Use the **AutoFill** feature to copy this formula to cells **D3 and D4** (or further if you have more kinds of fencing listed).
35. Save your work.
36. To create a chart, click the **column heading A** to select (highlight) the entire column.
37. Hold down the **Control key** on your keyboard.
38. Click the **column heading D** to select (highlight) the entire column as well.
39. Click the **Chart Wizard** button on the Standard toolbar.
40. At the **Chart Wizard – Step 1 of 4 – Chart Type** window, click on the **Standard Types** tab to bring it to the forefront, if necessary.
41. At the **Chart type** menu, click **Bar**.
42. At the **Chart sub-type** menu, click the **Clustered bar with 3-D visual effect**—the first one in the second row.
43. Click **Next**.
44. At the **Chart Wizard – Step 2 of 4 – Chart Source Data** window, click **Next**.
45. At the **Chart Wizard – Step 3 of 4 – Chart Options** window, click on the Titles tab to bring it to the forefront, if necessary.

46. Click in the **Chart title textbox** and type the following: **Puppy Play Area Fencing Costs**
47. Click in the **Category (X)** axis textbox and type the following: **Type of Fence**
48. Click in the **Value (Z)** axis textbox and type the following: **Cost**
49. Click the **Legend tab** to bring it to the forefront.
50. Click in the **Show legend** box to deselect it, removing the check mark from the box and the legend from the chart.
51. Click **Next**.
52. At the **Chart Wizard – Step 4 of 4 – Chart Location** window, click **As new sheet.**
53. Click in the **As new sheet** textbox and type the following: **Puppy Play Area Fencing Costs**
54. Click **Finish**.
55. The **Puppy Play Area Fencing Costs** chart now appears on its own worksheet.
56. Save your work.
57. Print the chart.
58. Exit *Microsoft Excel*.

Assessment

- Have each team of students write a two-page **Puppy Play Area Report**. In their report, each team should include background information about their puppy, the puppy's need for an adequate play area (including the perimeter), a summary of the fencing information they collected, the results of their cost calculations, and their final recommendation for fencing purchases. Encourage students to copy and paste their charts into the report.

Extension

- Have each team of students build a 3D model (to scale) of their puppy play area, including fencing, a puppy, grass, trees, etc.
- Have students research various dog breeds and their physical needs. Have students compile a list of care considerations for their new puppy.

Related CD Files

- **Puppy Play Area.xls** (a copy of the **Puppy Play Area** workbook file used in this student lesson)
- Sample **Puppy Play Area Data Organizer** (a copy of the Sample **Puppy Play Area Data Organizer** referred to in this student lesson)
- **Puppy Play Area Data Organizer** (a copy of the **Puppy Play Area Data Organizer** displayed to in this student lesson)

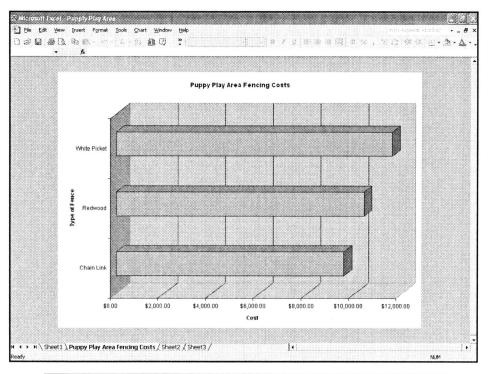

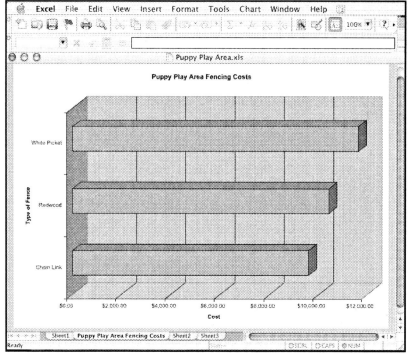

Sample Puppy Play Area Data Organizer

	Lumberyards or Home Improvement Stores			
Types of Fencing ▼				
				Cost Per Foot ◄

Sample Puppy Play Area Data Organizer

	Lumberyards or Home Improvement Stores			
Types of Fencing ▼				
				Cost Per Foot ◄

Currency Conversions
Grades 3-8

Lesson Summary

In this lesson, students pretend they are from different countries, traveling on a tour of the United States. Their last stop before returning home is Walt Disney World in Orlando, Florida. Students buy souvenirs and compare the costs in U. S. dollars to the currencies of their countries. Using a *Microsoft Excel* workbook, students enter the prices of the souvenirs, such as sweatshirts and Mickey Mouse ears. Using *Microsoft Excel* formulas, they convert the prices from U. S. dollars to the other international currencies.

Curriculum Content
- Discovering and "exploring" other countries
- Discovering other currencies
- Calculating exchange rates

Computer Skills
- Spreadsheet text entry
- Spreadsheet data entry
- Spreadsheet simple formatting
- Spreadsheet foreign currency displays

Materials
- **Travel Mates Money and Fact Finder**
- **Currency Exchange Rates**

Before the Computer

- Individual, pairs, or small groups of students can do this lesson, so vary the number of countries and currencies students investigate accordingly. Although current exchange rates are available at banks, in newspapers, and on the Internet, you will find a **Currency Exchange Rates** table near the end of this lesson.

- Discuss with students the concept of using different types of money if they travel to or live in foreign countries. Using the **Travel Mates Money and Fact Finder**, have students research and record the currency denominations for up to fifteen countries. Students can also add interesting facts they learn about the countries to share with the class.

- Have your students been to Disney World or a similar theme park? Discuss with students the types of souvenirs they purchased and their approximate costs. Have students select three souvenirs for use in the **Currency Conversions** workbook, such as a sweatshirt, a Winnie the Pooh™ bear, and Mickey Mouse™ ears. Also, have students select three countries (other than the United States) for use in the Coin Conversions workbook. We used Ireland, South Africa, and Japan.

At the Computer

1. Launch *Microsoft Excel.*
2. Click in cell **A1** and type the following: **Souvenirs**
3. Click in cell **B1** and type the following: **U.S. Dollars**
4. Click in cell **C1** and type a foreign country and its currency, such as **South African Rand**.
5. Click in cell **D1** and type another foreign country and its currency, such as **Japanese Yen**.
6. Click in cell **E1** and type another foreign country and its currency, such as **Indian Rupee**.
7. Continue in this manner until you enter all the foreign countries and their currencies that you wish.
8. Click in the **row heading 1** to select (highlight) the entire row.
9. Click the **Bold** button on the Formatting toolbar.
10. Click the **Center** button on the Formatting toolbar.
11. When the entire row is still selected, adjust the column widths to accommodate the length of text displayed. Click **Format** on the Menu bar.
12. Click **Column.**

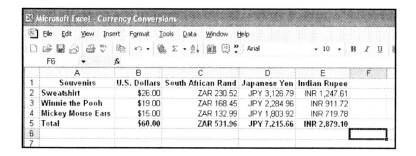

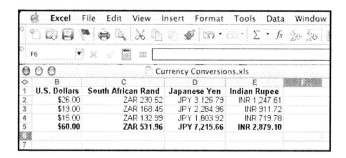

13. Click **AutoFit Selection**.

14. Click in cell **A2** and type the name of your first souvenir, such as **Sweatshirt**.

15. Click in cell **A3** and type the name of your second souvenir, such as **Winnie the Pooh**.

16. Click in cell **A4** and type the name of your third souvenir, such as **Mickey Mouse Ears**.

17. Click on the **column heading A** to select (highlight) the entire column.

18. Click the **Bold** button on the Formatting toolbar **twice**.

19. While the entire column is still selected, adjust the column width to accommodate the length of the text displayed. Click **Format** on the Menu bar.

20. Click **Column**.

21. Click **AutoFit Selection**.

22. To format column B for U.S. currency, click the **column heading B** to select (highlight) the entire column.

23. Click **Format** on the Menu bar.

24. Click **Cells**.

25. At the Format Cells dialog box, click the **Number** tab to bring it to the forefront, if necessary.
26. Click **Currency**.
27. Click **OK**.
28. To format column C for South African currency, click the **column heading C** to select (highlight) the entire column.
29. Click **Format** on the Menu bar.
30. Click **Cells**.
31. At the Format Cells dialog box, click the **Number** tab to bring it to the forefront, if necessary.
32. Click **Currency**.
33. Click the **Symbol** list arrow and scroll down to the currency symbol for the South African Rand, which is ZAR.
34. Click **ZAR**.
35. Click **OK**.
36. To format column D for Japanese currency, click the **column heading D** to select (highlight) the entire column.
37. Click **Format** on the Menu bar.
38. Click **Cells**.
39. At the Format Cells dialog box, click the **Number** tab to bring it to the forefront, if necessary.
40. Click **Currency**.
41. Click the **Symbol** list arrow and scroll down to the currency symbol for the Japanese Yen, which is JPY.
42. Click **JPY**.
43. Click **OK**.
44. To format column E for Indian currency, click the **column heading E** to select (highlight) the entire column.
45. Click **Format** on the Menu bar.
46. Click **Cells**.
47. At the Format Cells dialog box, click the **Number** tab to bring it to the forefront, if necessary.
48. Click **Currency**.
49. Click the **Symbol** list arrow and scroll down to the currency symbol for the Indian Rupee, which is INR.
50. Click **INR**.
51. Click **OK**.

52. Click in cell **B2** and enter the price of the first souvenir in U.S. Dollars, such as 26. Just enter the numeric value. Since you formatted the column for U.S. Dollars, *Microsoft Excel* will automatically add the dollar sign, add the decimal point, and right align the number.

53. Click in cell **B3** and enter the price of your second souvenir in U.S. dollars, such as **19**.

54. Click in cell **B4** and enter the price of your third souvenir in U.S. dollars, such as **14**.

55. To determine how many South African Rand it costs to purchase the first souvenir, look at the **Currency Exchange Rates** table. Note that the conversion rate is 8.8660.

56. Click in cell **C2**.

57. Type the following formula: **=B2*8.8660**

58. Click the **Enter** button to the left of the formula bar to accept the formula you entered.

59. Use the **AutoFill feature** to copy the exchange rate formula down to cells **C3 and C4**.

60. To determine how many Japanese Yen it costs to purchase the first souvenir, look at the **Currency Exchange Rate** table. Note that the conversion rate is 120.261.

61. Click in cell **D2**.

62. Enter the following formula: **=B2*120.261**

63. Click the **Enter** button to the left of the formula bar to accept the formula you entered.

64. Use the **AutoFill feature** to copy the exchange rate formula down to cells **D3 and D4**.

65. To determine how many Indian Rupees it costs to purchase the first souvenir, look at the **Currency Exchange Rate** table. Note that the conversion rate is 47.985.

66. Click in cell **E2**.

67. Enter the following formula: **=B2*47.985**

68. Click the **Enter** button to the left of the formula bar to accept the formula you entered.

69. Use the **AutoFill feature** to copy the exchange rate formula down to cells **E3 and E4**.

70. To see the dramatic differences among currencies, click in cell **A5** and type the following: **Total**

71. Click in cell **B5**.

72. Click the **AutoSum** button on the Standard toolbar.

73. Click on the **Enter** button to the left of the formula bar to accept this formula.

74. Click in cell **C5**.

75. Click the **AutoSum** button on the Standard toolbar.

76. Click on the **Enter** button to the left of the formula bar to accept this formula.

77. Click in cell **D5**.

78. Click the **AutoSum** button on the Standard toolbar.

79. Click on the **Enter** button to the left of the formula bar to accept this formula.

80. Click in cell **E5**.

81. Click the **row heading 5** to select (highlight) the entire row.

82. Click the **Bold** button on the Formatting toolbar **twice**.

83. Save your work.

84. Print the worksheet.

Assessment

- Have students discuss what countries' currencies might make them look like millionaires and what countries' currencies might make them look like paupers.

- To determine if students can apply this knowledge, have them calculate the estimated cost of a dinner at a restaurant at Walt Disney World in the currencies of the United States and two foreign countries.

Extension

- Have students create a budget for a weekend trip to Walt Disney World for someone visiting from Norway.

Related CD Files

- **Currency Conversions.xls** (a copy of the **Currency Conversions** workbook file used in this student lesson)

- **Travel Mates Money and Fact Finder.doc** (a copy of the **Travel Mates Money and Fact Finder** referred to in this student lesson—a *Microsoft Word* file)

- **Currency Exchange Rates.xls** (a copy of the **Currency Exchange Rates** displayed in this student lesson)

Travel Mates Money and Fact Finder				
Country	**Currency**	**Fun Fact 1**	**Fun Fact 2**	**Fun Fact 3**

Currency Exchange Rates

Symbol	Country (Currency)	Rate
ARP	Argentina (Peso)	3.4554
AUD	Australia (Dollar)	1.7756
BSD	Bahamas (Dollar)	1.0000
BRL	Brazil (Real)	3.5046
CAD	Canada (Dollar)	1.5480
CLP	Chile (Peso)	706.20
CNY	China (Renminbi)	8.2781
COP	Colombia (Peso)	2824.8
DKK	Denmark (Krone)	7.2101
EUR	Europe (Euro)	0.9705
FJD	Fiji Islands (Dollar)	2.0681
GHC	Ghana (Cedi)	8322.6
GBP	Great Britain (Pound)	0.6264
HNL	Honduras (Lempira)	16.900
HKD	Hong Kong (Dollar)	7.7988
ISK	Iceland (Krona)	82.209
INR	India (Rupee)	47.985
IDR	Indonesia (Rupiah)	8896.6
ILS	Israel (Shekel)	4.7793
JPY	Japan (Yen)	120.261
MYR	Malaysia (Ringgit)	3.7997
MXP	Mexico (New Peso)	10.2044
MAD	Morocco (Dirham)	10.3200
NZD	New Zealand (Dollar)	1.9338
NOK	Norway (Krone)	7.0492
PKR	Pakistan (Rupee)	58.305
PAB	Panama (Balboa)	1.0000
PEN	Peru (New Sol)	3.4983
PHP	Philippines (Peso)	53.508
RUR	Russia (Rouble)	31.813

Currency Exchange Rates

Symbol	Country (Currency)	Rate
ARP	Argentina (Peso)	3.4554
SGD	Singapore (Dollar)	1.7380
ZAR	South Africa (Rand)	8.8660
KRW	South Korea (Won)	1200.93
LKR	Sri Lanka (Rupee)	96.629
SEK	Sweden (Krona)	8.8660
CHF	Switzerland (Franc)	1.4088
TWD	Taiwan (Dollar)	34.747
THB	Thailand (Baht)	42.917
TTD	Trinidad/Tobago (Dollar)	6.1600
TND	Tunisia (Dinar)	1.3398
TRL	Turkey (Lira)	1.6775
USD	United States (Dollar)	1.0000
VEB	Venezuela (Bolivar)	1377.22

Presidential Parade
Grades 4-8

Lesson Summary

"Hail to the chief!" Every four years, our country holds a president election. Have you ever wondered if there is a relationship between the age of an elected president and the number of electoral votes he received? Or is there a relationship between a president's age at death and the number of months served? In this lesson, students gather data about the presidents and use a *Microsoft Excel* worksheet to explore these and other questions.

Curriculum Concepts

- Examining the executive branch of government
- Examining the electoral process

Computer Skills

- Spreadsheet text entry
- Spreadsheet data entry
- Spreadsheet simple formatting
- Charting
- Chart formatting

Materials

- **Presidential Data Organizer**
- **Presidential Data Organizer Sample**

Before the Computer

- Discuss the electoral process with students. Explain how a president can win an election and not receive the most votes.
- Brainstorm with students the different types of data they might collect about the presidents, such as number of months in office, number of electoral votes received, age when elected, age at death, and more.
- Divide students into small groups. Have each group select six or more presidents to investigate.
- Using the **Presidential Data Organizer**, have students gather information about their selected presidents.
- Display the **Presidential Data Organizer Sample**, if necessary, to provide an example for students.

At the Computer

1. Launch *Microsoft Excel*.
2. Click in cell **A1** and type the following: **President**
3. Click in cell **B1** and type the following: **Months in Office**
4. Click in cell **C1** and type the following: **Electoral Votes**
5. Click in cell **D1** and type the following: **Age at Election**
6. Click in cell **E1** and type the following: **Age at Death**
7. To format the column headings and adjust the column widths, click the **row heading 1** to select (highlight) the entire row.
8. Click **Bold** on the Formatting toolbar.
9. Click **Center** on the Formatting toolbar.
10. Click **Format** on the Menu bar.
11. Click **Column**.
12. Click **AutoFit Selection**.
13. Click in cell **A2** and type the name of the first president, such as **George Washington**.
14. Click in cell **A3** and type the name of the second president, such as **Thomas Jefferson**.
15. Click in cell **A4** and type the name of the third president, such as **Abraham Lincoln**.

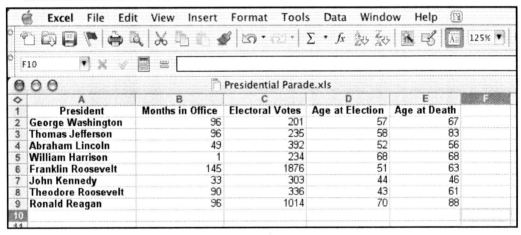

16. Continue in this manner until the names of the remaining presidents are entered in column A.

17. To format the row headings and adjust the column width, click the **column heading A** to select (highlight) the entire row.

18. Click **Bold** on the Formatting toolbar twice.

19. Click **Format** on the Menu bar.

20. Click **Column**.

21. Click **AutoFit Selection**.

22. Enter the number of months each president was in office in cells **B2 through B9**.

23. Enter the number of electoral votes each president received in cells **C2 through C9**.

24. Enter the age at which each president was elected in cells **D2 through D9**.
25. Enter the age at which each president died in cells **E2 through E9**.
26. Save your work.
27. To create a chart that displays the relationship between each president's age when elected and age at death, click the **column heading A** to select (highlight) all the presidents' names.
28. Hold down the **Control key** on your keyboard and click on column **headings D and E** as well.
29. Click the **Chart Wizard** button on the Standard toolbar.
30. At the **Chart Wizard – Step 1 of 4 – Chart Type** dialog box, click the Standard Types tab to bring it to the forefront, if necessary.
31. At the **Chart type** menu, select **Line**.
32. At the **Chart sub-type menu**, select the **Line with markers displayed at each data value chart**—the first one in the second row.
33. Click **Next**.
34. At the **Chart Wizard – Step 2 of 4 – Chart Source Data** dialog box, click **Next**.
35. At the **Chart Wizard – Step 3 of 4 – Chart Options** dialog box, click on the **Titles** tab to bring it to the forefront, if necessary.
36. Click in the **Chart title** textbox and type the following: **Presidential Ages at Election and Death**
37. Click in the **Category (X)** axis textbox and type the following: **Presidents**
38. Click in the **Value (Y)** axis textbox and type the following: **Ages**
39. Click on the **Legends** tab to bring it to the forefront.
40. Under the **Placement** menu, select **Bottom**.
41. Click on the **Data Labels** tab to bring it to the forefront.
42. Under the **Label Contains** menu, select **Value**.
43. Click **Next**.
44. At the **Chart Wizard – Step 4 of 4 – Chart Location** dialog box, select **As new sheet**.
45. Click in the **As new sheet textbox** and type the following: **Presidential Ages**
46. Click **Finish**.
47. The **Presidential Ages** chart should now appear on its own worksheet in your workbook.
48. Save your work.

49. To format the data values, double-click on any value on the Age at Election line.
50. At the **Format Data Labels** dialog box, click **Bold** under **Font style**.
51. Click **OK**.
52. Double click on any value on the **Age at Death** line.
53. At the **Format Data Labels** dialog box, click **Bold** under **Font** style.
54. Click **OK**.
55. Save your work.
56. Print the chart.
57. Print the chart to share with your students.
58. Continue creating additional charts that display different relationships or exit *Microsoft Excel*.

Assessment

- Using the **Presidential Ages** chart, as well as other charts you may have created, have students discuss the displayed findings, such as the president who lived the longest after he was elected, the presidents who died while in office, etc.

Extension

- Have students gather information about the number of popular votes the presidents received. Compare the popular votes with the electoral votes. Did any of the presidents the students chose to investigate receive the most popular votes but lose the election based upon electoral votes?

- Have students investigate and then discuss how the change in the voting system in our early history affected subsequent elections? (Originally, the candidate with the highest number of votes became the president and the candidate with the second highest number of votes became the vice president.)

Related CD Files

- **Presidential Parade.xls** (a copy of the Presidential Parade workbook used in this student lesson)

- **Presidential Data Organizer.doc** (a copy of the Presidential Data Organizer referred to in this student lesson—a *Microsoft Word* file)

- **Presidential Data Organizer Sample.doc** (a copy of the **Presidential Data Organizer Sample** referred to in this student lesson—a *Microsoft Word* file)

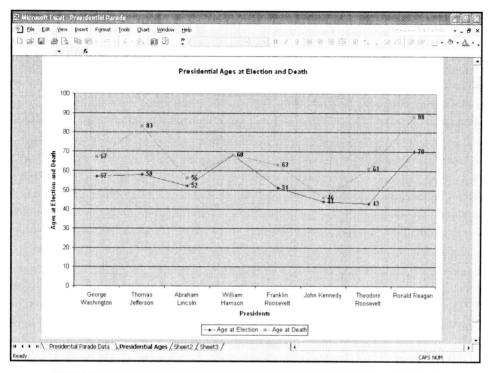

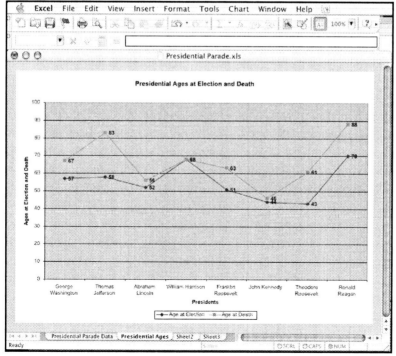

Presidential Data Organizer				
President	**Months in Office**	**Electoral Votes**	**Age at Election**	**Age at Death**

Presidential Data Organizer

President	Months in Office	Electoral Votes	Age at Election	Age at Death
George Washington	96	201	57	67
Thomas Jefferson	96	325	58	83
William Harrison	1	234	68	68
Abraham Lincoln	49	392	52	56
Theodore Roosevelt	90	336	43	61
Franklin D. Roosevelt	145	1876	51	63
John F. Kennedy	33	303	44	46

Population Explosion
Grades 5–8

Lesson Summary

We are all aware that the world population is growing, but will the growth ever slow down? Questions about whether there will be enough food and water to support the world are constantly being asked and analyzed by governments and people all around the world. In this lesson, students compare the population of the six inhabited continents for 1950, 1970, 1990, and 2010 (projected) using a column chart. Then students use a pie chart to examine the world population as a whole. Students also look a population growth over time using a line chart.

Curriculum Content

- Researching a variety of populations
- Naming continents
- Determining continent populations
- Interpreting charted data

Computer Skills

- Charting (column, pie, and line)

Materials

- **Population Data Organizer**
- **Population Explosion**

Before the Computer

- Have students guess the populations of their school, city, state, country, world, and other selected areas of interest. Using the **Population Data Organizer**, have students use a variety of resources (interviews, textbooks, reference books, the Internet, etc.) to find out the actual populations of the areas listed.

- Discuss with students the term growth rate and its potential impact on the world's resources.

- Have students name the seven continents of the world (Africa, Antarctica, Asia, Europe, North America, Australia, and South America) and decide which are inhabited (all but Antarctica are considered inhabited).

- After finding each inhabited continent on a map, have students guess which continents have the greatest population and growth rates. Explain to students that population data can be displayed in charts to help us compare populations, see growth rates, and predict trends that may affect our future.

- Discuss with students the three most commonly used charts—column or bar charts, pie charts, and line charts—and how they are used to display different types of data.

Note: At the computer you and your students will create all three types of charts from population data provided in the **Population Explosion** workbook—a file that you will find on the CD in the back of the book.

At the Computer

1. Launch *Microsoft Excel*.
2. Insert the **Excel for Terrified Teachers CD** in the CD-ROM drive of your computer.
3. Click **File** on the Menu bar.
4. Click **Open**.
5. At the **Open** dialog box, click the **Look in** list arrow and navigate to your CD drive.
6. From the list of files on the CD, select **Population Explosion.xls**.
7. Click the **Open** button.
8. Save this file to your computer system.
9. To create a column chart that displays each continent's population in 1990, select (highlight) the names of the continents in cells **B3 through B8**.
10. Hold down the **Control key** on your keyboard and select (highlight) the 1990 population values of the continents in cells **F3 through F8**.
11. Click the **Chart Wizard** button on the Standard toolbar.
12. At the **Chart Wizard – Step 1 of 4 – Chart Type** dialog box, click on the **Standard Types** tab to bring it to the forefront, if necessary.
13. At the **Chart type** menu, select **Column**.

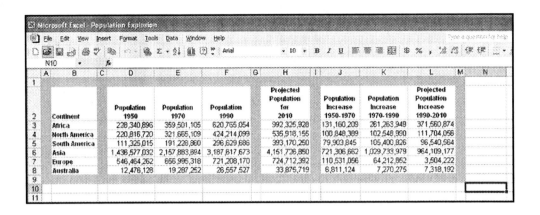

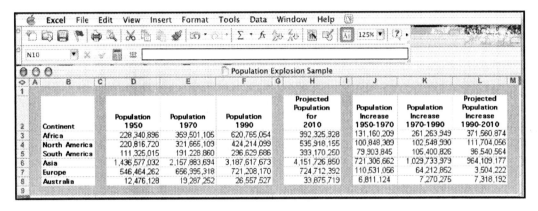

14. At the **Chart sub-type** menu, select the **Clustered column with 3-D visual effect** chart—the first one in the second row.

15. Click the **Next** button to continue.

16. At the **Chart Wizard – Step 2 of 4 – Chart Source Data** dialog box, click **Next**.

17. At the **Chart Wizard – Step 3 of 4 – Chart Options** window, click on the **Titles** tab to bring it to the forefront, if necessary.

18. Click in the **Chart title** textbox and type the following: **Continent Populations in 1990**

19. Click in the **Category (X) axis** textbox and type the following: **Continents**

20. Click in the **Value (Z) axis** textbox and type the following: **Population**

21. Click the **Legends** tab to bring it to the forefront.

22. Click **Show Legend** to deselect it. The legend will disappear from your chart display.

23. Click the **Data Labels** tab to bring it to the forefront.

24. Under the **Label Contains** menu, select **Value**.

25. Click the **Next** button to continue.

26. At the **Chart Wizard – Step 4 of 4 – Chart Location** dialog box, select **As new sheet**.

27. Click in the **As new sheet textbox** and type the following: **Continent Populations in 1990**.

28. Click the **Finish** button.

29. The **Continent Populations in 1990** column chart now appears on its own worksheet in your workbook.

30. Save your work.

31. Print the chart.

32. To create a pie chart that displays each continent's population as a percentage of the world's population in 1990, click the **Population Data** workbook tab to return your worksheet.

33. The **values in columns B and F** should still be selected (highlighted). If they are not, reselect them for charting.

34. Click the **Chart Wizard** button on the Standard toolbar.

35. At the **Chart Wizard – Step 1 of 4 – Chart Type** dialog box, click the Standard Types to bring it to the forefront, if necessary.

36. At the **Chart type** menu, select **Pie**.

37. At the **Chart sub-type** menu, select the **Exploded pie with 3-D visual effect chart**—the second one in the second row.

38. Click the **Next** button to continue.

39. At the **Chart Wizard – Step 2 of 4 – Chart Source Data** dialog box, click **Next** to continue.

40. At the **Chart Wizard – Step 3 of 4 – Chart Options** window, click the **Titles** tab to bring it to the forefront, if necessary.

41. Click in the **Chart title** textbox and type the following: **World Population by Continent in 1990**

42. Click on the **Legends** tab to bring it to the forefront.

43. Click **Show Legend** to deselect it. The legend disappears from your chart display.

44. Click on the **Data Labels** tab to bring it to the forefront.

45. Under the **Label Contains** menu, select **Category Name**.

46. Also under the **Label Contains** menu, select **Percentage**.

47. Click the **Next** button to continue.

48. At the **Chart Wizard – Step 4 of 4 – Chart Location** dialog box, select **As new sheet**.

49. Click in the As new sheet textbox and type the following: **World Population in 1990**

50. Click the **Finish** button.

51. **The World Population** pie chart now appears on its own worksheet in your workbook.

52. Save your work.

53. Print the pie chart.

54. To create a line chart that displays each continent's population growth over time, click the **Population Data** workbook tab to return your worksheet.

55. Select (highlight) the **Continent** column—**cells B2 through B8**.

56. Hold down the **Control key** on your keyboard and select (highlight) the **Population 1950** column—cells **D2 through D8**, the **Population 1970** column—cells **E2 through E8**, and the **Population 1990** column—cells **F2 through F8** as well.

57. Click the **Chart Wizard** button on the Standard toolbar.

58. At the **Chart Wizard – Step 1 of 4 – Chart Type** dialog box, click the Standard Types tab to bring it to the forefront, if necessary.

59. At the **Chart type** menu, select **Line**.

60. At the **Chart sub-type** menu, select the **Line with markers displayed at each data value chart**—the first one in the second row.

61. Click the **Next** button to continue.

62. At the **Chart Wizard – Step 2 of 4 – Chart Source Data** dialog box, click the **Data Range** tab to bring it to the forefront, if necessary.

63. Under **Series in**, click **Row**.

64. Click the **Next** button to continue.

65. At the **Chart Wizard – Step 3 of 4 – Chart Options** dialog box, click on the **Titles** tab to bring it to the forefront, if necessary.

66. Click in the **Chart title** textbox and type the following: **Population Growth**

67. Click in the **Category (X) axis** textbox and type the following: **Time**
68. Click in the **Value (Y) axis** textbox and type the following: **Population**
69. Click the **Legend** tab to bring it to the forefront.
70. Under **Placement**, click **Bottom**.
71. Click the **Next** button to continue.
72. At the **Chart Wizard – Step 4 of 4 – Chart Location** dialog box, select **As new sheet**.
73. Click in the **As new sheet textbox** and type the following: **Population Growth**
74. Click the **Finish** button.
75. The **Growth Rate** chart now appears on its own worksheet in your workbook.
76. Save your work.
77. Print the line chart.
78. Continue making other charts that display the population data in a variety of ways or exit *Microsoft Excel.*

Assessment

- Referring to the column chart, the pie chart, and the line chart that were generated during this lesson, discuss with students the answers to the following questions:

    1. Which continent's population seems to be growing faster than the others?
    2. On which continents does the growth rate seem to be neither increasing nor decreasing, but rather remaining about the same?
    3. What factors (political, economic, geographic, etc.) might be contributing to the growth rate for each of the continents?
    - Have students determine other ways they can select, chart, and display the population data, such as the growth rate for just one continent over time, the projected population of the world in 2010, and more. Let students create and display their charts in the classroom.

Extension

- Have students enter and chart the data collected in their Population Data Organizers, such as the growth of their school's population over time.
- Discuss with students the effects of birth rates and mortality rates on world population.
- Have students complete a research project on a continent of their choice.

Related CD Files

- **Population Explosion.xls** (a copy of the **Population Explosion** workbook referred to in this student lesson)
- **Population Explosion Sample.xls** (a sample copy of the workbook used in this student lesson that displays the completed column, pie, and line charts)
- **Population Explosion Data Organizer.doc** (a copy of the **Population Explosion Data Organizer** referred to in this student lesson—a *Microsoft Word* file)

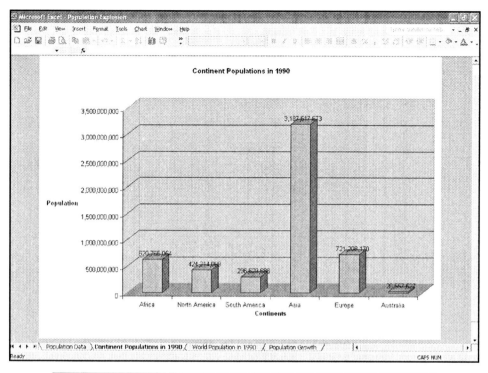

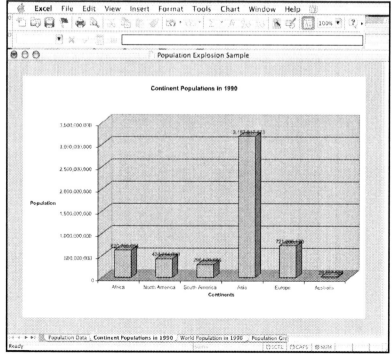

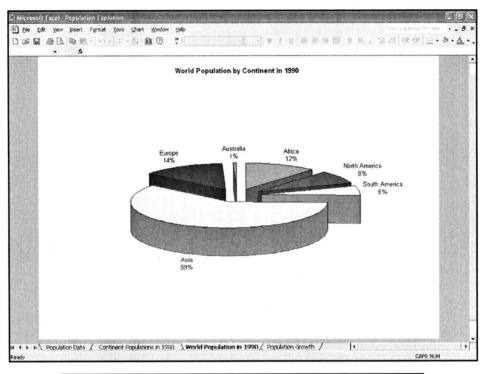

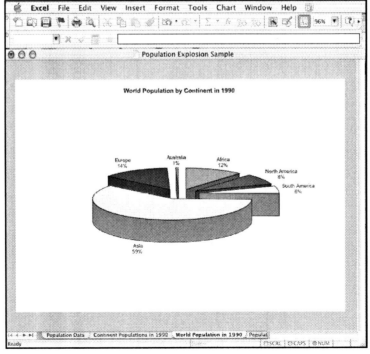

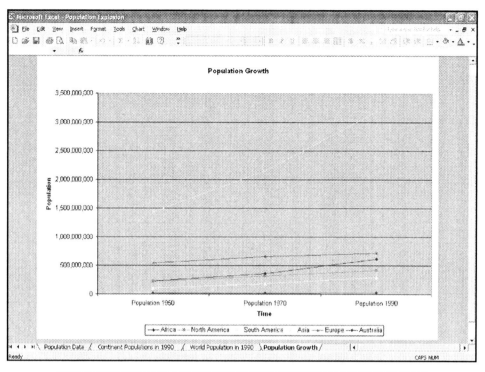

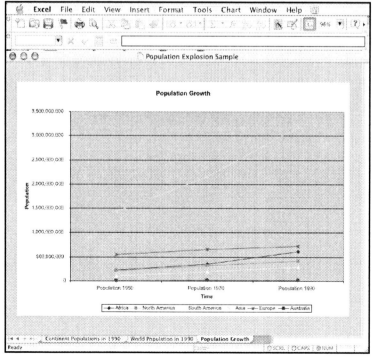

Population Data Organizer

	Estimated	Actual
The population of my school ten years ago		
The population of my school five years ago		
The population of my school today		
The population of my city		
The population of my state		
The population of my country		
The population of the world		
Other area:		
Other area:		
Other area:		

Weekend Watch
Grades 3–8

Lesson Summary

Most children watch over ten hours of television each week, but what kinds of shows are they watching? In this lesson, students keep a log of the shows they view from Friday afternoon through Sunday night. This information is then categorized by program type and analyzed in terms of hours per type in a *Microsoft Excel* worksheet. Findings are displayed using charts.

Curriculum Content

- Classifying media
- Collecting data (documenting television viewing habits)
- Interpreting chart data

Computer Skills

- Spreadsheet text entry
- Spreadsheet data entry
- Spreadsheet simple formatting
- Spreadsheet simple formula
- Charting

Before the Computer

- Discuss with students the types of television programs that they watch, such as cartoons, sitcoms, sports, movies, dramas, etc.
- Have students select five categories in which to classify the television programs they watch.
- Have students keep a record of their television viewing habits over a weekend using the **Weekend Watch Television Log.**

Materials

- **Weekend Watch Television Log**

At the Computer

1. Launch *Microsoft Excel.*
2. Click in cell **B1** and type the first category, such as **Cartoons**.
3. Click in cell **C1** and type the second category, such as **Sitcoms**.
4. Click in cell **D1** and type the third category, such as **Sports**.
5. Click in cell **E1** and type the fourth category, such as **Movies**.
6. Click in cell **F1** and type the fifth category, such as **Dramas**.
7. Click in cell **G1** and type the following: **Total**To format the column labels, click the **row heading 1** to highlight (select) the entire row.
8. Click the **Bold** button on the Formatting toolbar.
9. Click the **Center** button on the Formatting toolbar.
10. While the row is still selected, adjust the column widths. Click **Format** on the Menu bar.
11. Click **Column**.
12. Click **AutoFit Selection**.
13. Working with your first group of students, click in cell **A2** and type the first student's name, such as **Melissa**.
14. Click in cell **A3** and type the second student's name, such as **Eric**.
15. Click in cell **A4** and type the third student's name, such as **Jose**.
16. Click in cell **A5** and type the fourth student's name, such as **Trina**.
17. Click in cell **A6** and type the following: **Total**
18. Click on the **column heading A** to select (highlight) the entire column.
19. Click the **Bold** button on the Formatting toolbar.
20. While the column is still selected adjust the column width, if necessary.
21. Enter the number of hours that each student in the first group watched the categorized television programs in cells **B2 through F5**.
22. Using the **AutoSum feature**, click in cell **G2** and calculate the total number of hours the first student watched television.
23. Using the **AutoFill feature**, apply this formula to cells **G3 through G5**.
24. Click the **column heading G** to select (highlight) the entire column.
25. Click the **Bold** button on the Formatting toolbar **twice**.

26. Using the **AutoSum feature**, click in cell **B6** and calculate the total number of hours the students watched cartoons.

27. Using the **AutoFill feature**, apply this formula to cells C6 through F6.

28. Click the **row heading 6** to select (highlight) the entire row.

29. Click the **Bold** button on the Formatting toolbar **twice**.

30. Save your work.

31. To create a chart that displays this group of students' television viewing over the weekend, click the **row heading 1** to select (highlight) the entire row.

32. Hold down the **Control key** on your keyboard and click the **row heading 6** to highlight (select) the entire row as well.

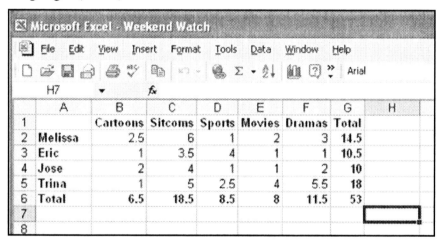

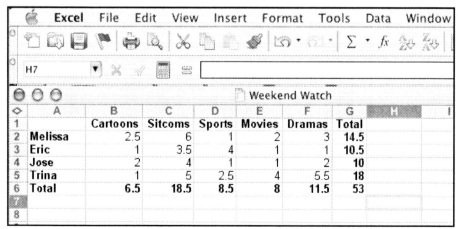

33. Click the **Chart Wizard** button on the Standard toolbar.

34. At the **Chart Wizard – Step 1 of 4 – Chart Type** dialog box, click on the **Standard Types** tab to bring it to the forefront, if necessary.

35. At the **Chart type** menu, select **Column**.

36. At the **Chart sub-type** menu, select the **Clustered column with a 3-D visual effect chart**—the first one in the second row.

37. Click the **Next** button to continue.

38. At the **Chart Wizard – Step 2 of 4 – Chart Source Data** dialog box, click **Next** to continue.

39. At the **Chart Wizard – Step 3 of 4 – Chart Options** dialog box, click on the **Titles** tab to bring it to the forefront, if necessary.

40. Click in the **Chart title** textbox and type the following: **Weekend Watch**.

41. Click in the **Category (X) axis** textbox and type the following: **Television Programs**

42. Click in the **Value (Z) axis** textbox and type the following: **Hours Watching Television**

43. Click the **Legends** tab to bring it to the forefront.

44. Click **Show Legend** to deselect it. The legend will disappear from your chart display.

45. Click the **Next** button to continue.

46. At the **Chart Wizard – Step 4 of 4 – Chart Location** dialog box, select **As new sheet**.

47. Click in the **As new sheet** textbox and type the following: **Weekend Watch**

48. Click the **Finish** button.

49. The **Weekend Watch** chart now appears on its own worksheet in your workbook.

50. Save your work.

51. Print your chart.

52. Print the chart to share with your students.

53. Chart the data another way, chart the data with another small group, or exit *Microsoft Excel*.

Assessment

- After viewing their charts, have students draw conclusions about the type and amount of television programming that they watch.
- Discuss whether students watch too much television, whether they have similar viewing habits, etc.

Extension

- Collect, enter, and chart data about students' television viewing habits during the school week. Compare these to their weekend television viewing habits.

Related CD Files

- **Weekend Watch.xls** (a copy of the **Weekend Watch** workbook used in this student lesson)
- **Weekend Watch Television Log.doc** (a copy of the **Weekend Watch Television Log** referred to in this student lesson—a *Microsoft Word* file)

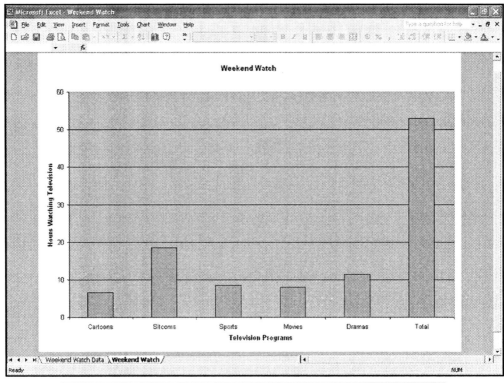

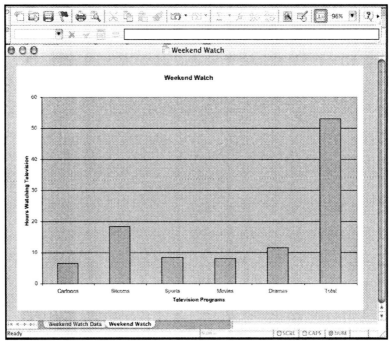

Weekend Watch Television Log

Day	Name of TV Show	Type of TV Show	Starting Time of TV Show	Ending Time of TV Show	Time TV Show Watched
				Total	

High Mountains and Low Valleys
Grades 5-8

Lesson Summary

What is the highest peak in South America? What is the lowest point in Australia? In this lesson, students compare the highest and the lowest elevations on each of the continents. The data on highest and lowest elevations for each continent are entered in a *Microsoft Excel* spreadsheet. Then students create line and bar graphs.

Curriculum Content

- Naming the continents
- "Exploring" the continents
- Researching the highest elevation points
- Researching the lowest elevation points
- Viewing topographical or contour maps
- Interpreting data

Computer Skills

- Spreadsheet text entry
- Spreadsheet data entry
- Spreadsheet simple formatting
- Charting

Materials

- **High Mountains and Low Valleys Data Organizer**
- **High Mountains and Low Valleys Answer Key**
- **High Mountains and Low Valleys Assessment**

Before the Computer

- Have students name the seven continents of the world (Africa, Antarctica, Asia, Australia, Europe, North America, and South America) and ask if any know the highest and lowest points on each continent.

- Show students topographical or contour maps of the world. Define elevation. Discuss the meaning of above sea level and below sea level.
- Define the mathematical way to write above sea level and below sea level, using the positive and negative signs.
- Using the Internet, world almanacs, or other fact books, have students complete the **High Mountains and Low Valleys Data Organizer**.

At the Computer

1. Launch *Microsoft Excel*.
2. Click in cell **A1** and type the following: **Continent**
3. Click in cell **B1** and type the following: **Highest Point**
4. Click in cell **C1** and type the following: **Height (Feet)**
5. Click in cell **D1** and type the following: **Lowest Point**
6. Click in cell **E1** and type the following: **Depth (Feet)**
7. To formatting the column labels, click in **row heading 1** to select (highlight) the entire row.
8. Click the **Bold** button on the Formatting toolbar.
9. Click the **Center** button on the Formatting toolbar.
10. To adjust the column widths, click **Format** on the Menu bar.
11. Click **Column**.
12. Click **AutoFit Selection**.
13. Click in cell **A2** and type the following: **North America**
14. Click in cell **A3** and type the following: **South America**
15. Click in cell **A4** and type the following: **Asia**
16. Click in cell **A5** and type the following: **Africa**
17. Click in cell **A6** and type the following: **Europe**
18. Click in cell **A7** and type the following: **Australia**
19. Click in cell **A8** and type the following: **Antarctica**
20. To format the row labels, click in **column heading A** to select (highlight) the entire column.
21. Click the **Bold** button on the Formatting toolbar **twice**.
22. To adjust the column width, click **Format** on the Menu bar.
23. Click **Column**.
24. In cells **B2 through B8**, type the highest point for each continent.
25. Adjust the width of **column B**.

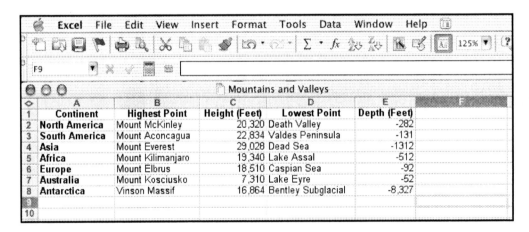

26. In cells **C2 through C8**, type the height (above sea level) for each of the highest points you typed in column B.
27. Adjust the width of **column C**.
28. In cells **D2 through D8**, type the lowest point for each continent.
29. Adjust the width of **column D**.
30. In cells **E2 through E8**, type the depth (below sea level) for each of the lowest points you typed in column D.
31. Adjust the width of **column E**, if necessary.
32. Save your work.

33. To create a line chart that displays the highest points for each continent, click on **column heading A**.
34. Hold down the **Control key** on your keyboard and click on **column headings B and C** as well.
35. Click the **Chart Wizard** button on the Standard toolbar.
36. At the **Chart Wizard – Step 1 of 4 – Chart Type** dialog box, click on the Standard Types tab to bring it to the forefront, if necessary.
37. At the **Chart type** menu, select **Line**.
38. At the **Chart sub-type** menu, select the **Line with markers displayed at each data value chart**—the first one in the second row.
39. Click the **Next** button to continue.
40. At the **Chart Wizard – Step 2 of 4 – Chart Source Data** dialog box, click **Next** to continue.
41. At the **Chart Wizard – Step 3 of 4 – Chart Options** window, click on the **Titles** tab to bring it to the forefront, if necessary.
42. Click in the **Chart title** textbox and type the following: **The Highest Points on Each Continent**
43. Click in the **Category (X) axis** textbox and type the following: **Continents and Points**
44. Click in the **Value (Y) axis** textbox and type the following: **Height in Feet**
45. Click in the **Legends** tab bringing it to the forefront.
46. Click **Show legend** to deselect it. The legend disappears from your chart display.
47. Click on the **Data Labels** tab to bring it to the forefront.
48. Under the **Label Contains** menu, select **Value**.
49. Click the **Next** button to continue.
50. At the **Chart Wizard – Step 4 of 4 – Chart Location** dialog box, select **As new sheet**.
51. Click in the **As new sheet** textbox and type the following: **Highest Points on Continents**
52. Click the **Finish** button.
53. **The Highest Point on Each Continent** line chart now appears on its own worksheet in your workbook.
54. Save your work.
55. Print the line chart.
56. Continue creating other charts to display height and depth information or exit *Microsoft Excel*.

Assessment

- Using research data, the **Mountains and Valleys** workbook, and **The Highest Point on Each Continent** chart, have students complete the **High Mountains and Low Valleys Assessment**.

Extension

- Create a line chart that displays **The Lowest Point on Each Continent** information.
- Create a line chart that displays heights and depths of all continents.
- Have students research to find the longest rivers, tallest waterfalls, or other geographic information for each continent.

Related CD Files

- **Mountains and Valleys.xls** (a copy of the **Mountains and Valleys** workbook used in this student lesson)
- **High Mountains and Low Valleys Data Organizer.doc** (a copy of the **High Mountains and Low Valleys Data Organizer** referred to in this lesson—a *Microsoft Word* file)
- **High Mountains and Low Valleys Assessment.doc** (a copy of the **High Mountains and Low Valleys Assessment** referred to in this lesson—a *Microsoft Word* file)

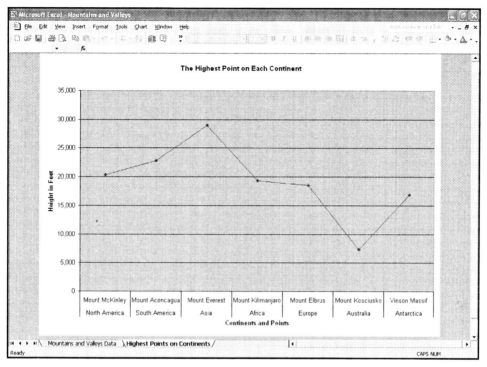

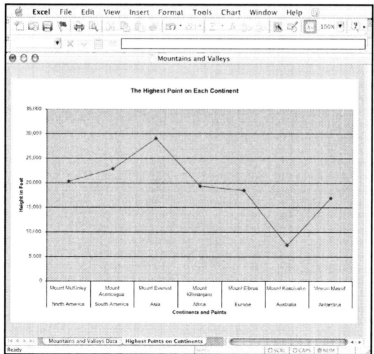

High Mountains and Low Valleys Data Organizer

Continent	Highest Point	Height (in feet above sea level)	Lowest Point	Depth (in feet below sea level)
North America				
South America				
Asia				
Africa				
Europe				
Australia				
Antarctica				

High Mountains and Low Valleys Data Organizer

Continent	Highest Point	Height (in feet above sea level)	Lowest Point	Depth (in feet below sea level)
North America	Mt. McKinley (Alaska)	20,320	Death Valley (California)	-282
South America	Mount Aconcagua (Argentina)	22,834	Valdes Peninsula (Argentina)	-131
Asia	Mount Everest (Nepal-Tibet)	29,028	Dead Sea (Israel-Jordan)	-1,312
Africa	Mount Kilimanjaro (Tanzania)	19,340	Lake Assal (Djibouti)	-512
Europe	Mount Elbrus (Russia)	18,510	Caspian Sea (Russia-Azerbaijan)	-92
Australia	Mount Kosciusko (New South Wales)	7,310	Lake Eyre (South Australia)	-52
Antarctica	Vinson Massif	16,864	Bentley Subglacial Trench	-8,327

	High Mountains and Low Valleys Assessment
	Directions: Using your research data, provide the following information about the highest and lowest points on the continents.
1.	**Rank the continents by highest elevation.** 1st 2nd 3rd 4th 5th 6th 7th
2.	**Rank the continents by greatest depth.** 1st 2nd 3rd 4th 5th 6th 7th
3.	**How much taller is Mount Everest than Mount Kilimanjaro?**
4.	**How much deeper is the Dead Sea than the Caspian Sea?**
5.	**Which continent has the greatest difference between its highest point and its lowest point?**
6.	**Which continent is projected to experience a decrease in growth rate from 1990 to 2010?**
7.	**Why may the Bentley Subglacial Trench not be the lowest point in Antarctica?**
8.	**List two resources for the information you provided.**

Sunrise and Sunset
Grades 3 and Up

Lesson Summary

In this lesson, students record sunrise and sunset times for five cities across the United States and display their findings using a line chart. Using a formula, students calculate the number of daylight hours for each city and compare the daylight hours using a column chart.

Curriculum Concepts

- Recording sunrise times
- Recording sunset times
- Calculating daylight hours
- Comparing daylight hours
- Interpreting charts

Computer Skills

- Spreadsheet text entry
- Spreadsheet data entry
- Spreadsheet simple formatting
- Spreadsheet simple formulas
- Charting

Materials

- **Sunrise and Sunset Data Organizer**

Before the Computer

- Discuss with students the meanings of the terms sunrise, sunset, and daylight.

- Ask students to predict what time the sun will rise and set tomorrow. Based upon these predictions, help student calculate the number of hours and minutes of daylight hours. (*Microsoft Excel* will do this during their actual activity.)

- If students have access to the Internet, let them choose five U.S. cities and use www.cnn.com as a resource for recording data in the **Sunrise and Sunset Data Organizer**.

- You may find that your local newspaper publishes sunrise and sunset information each day. If neither of these options is available to you, feel free to use the **Sunrise and Sunset Data** provided at the end of this lesson.

At the Computer

1. Launch *Microsoft Excel.*
2. Click in cell **A1** and type the following: **City and State**
3. Click in cell **B1** and type the following: **Sunrise**
4. Click in cell **C1** and type the following: **Sunset**
5. Click in cell **D1** and type the following: **Daylight Hours**
6. To format the column labels, click the **row heading 1** to select (highlight) the entire row.
7. Click the Bold button on the Formatting toolbar.
8. Click the **Center** button on the Formatting toolbar.
9. While the entire row is still selected, adjust the column widths. Click **Format** on the Menu bar.
10. Click **Column.**
11. Click **AutoFit Selection.**
12. Click in cell **A2** and enter the name of your first city and state abbreviation, such as **Las Cruces, NM.**
13. Click in cell **B2** and enter the name of your second city, such as **Hesperia, CA.**
14. Click in cell **C2** and enter the name of your third city and state abbreviation, such as **Brockton, MA.**
15. Click in cell **D2** and enter the name of your fourth city and state abbreviation, such as **Oklahoma City, OK.**
16. Click in cell **E2** and enter the name of your fifth city and state abbreviation, such as **Anchorage, AK.**
17. To format the row labels, click the **column heading A** to select (highlight) the entire column.
18. Click the **Bold** button on the Formatting toolbar.
19. While the entire column is selected, adjust the column width. Click **Format** on the Menu bar.
20. Click **Column.**
21. Click **AutoFit Selection.**

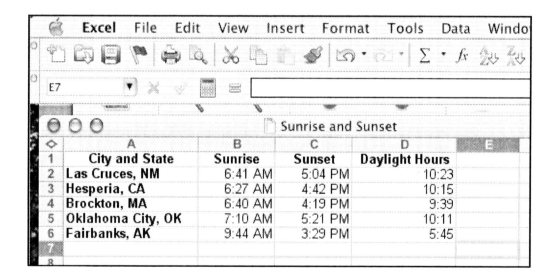

22. Before students enter sunrise and sunset times, formatting the cells for time. Select (highlight) cells **B2 through C6**, where time values will be entered.

23. Click **Format** on the Menu bar.

24. Click **Cells**.

25. At the **Format Cells** dialog box, click the **Number** tab to bring it to the forefront.

26. Under **Category**, click **Time**.

27. Under **Type**, click **1:30 PM**.
28. Click **OK**.
29. Enter the sunrise times for the listed cities in cells **B2 through B6**. Be sure to include AM in capital letters with no periods.
30. Enter the sunset times for the listed cities in cells **C2 through C6**. Be sure to include PM in capital letters with no periods.
31. To create a formula that will calculate the daylight hours, click in cell **D2**.
32. Type the following formula: **=C2-B2**
33. Click the **Enter** button to the left of the formula bar.
34. Using the **AutoFill feature**, click and drag the fill handle in cell **D2** down through cell **D6**.
35. Save your work.
36. To create a line chart that displays the sunrise and sunset times for the cities, select (highlight) cells **A1 through C6**.
37. Click the **Chart Wizard** button on the Standard toolbar.
38. At the **Chart Wizard – Step 1 of 4 – Chart Type** dialog box, click the **Standard Types** tab to bring it to the forefront, if necessary.
39. At the **Chart type** menu, select **Line**.
40. At the **Chart sub-type** menu, select the **Line with markers displayed at the data value chart**—the first one in the second row.
41. Click the **Next** button to continue.
42. At the **Chart Wizard – Step 2 of 4 – Chart Source Data** dialog box, click **Next** to continue.
43. At the **Chart Wizard – Step 3 of 4 – Chart Options** dialog box, click on the **Titles** tab to bring it to the forefront, if necessary.
44. Click in the **Chart title** textbox and type the following: **Sunrise and Sunset**
45. Click in the **Category (X) axis** textbox and type the following: **Cities and States**
46. Click in the **Value (Y) axis** textbox and type the following: **Time**
47. Click the **Legend** tab to bring it to the forefront.
48. Under **Placement**, click **Bottom**.
49. Click the **Next** button to continue.
50. At the **Chart Wizard – Step 4 of 4 – Chart Location** dialog box, click **As new sheet**.
51. Click in the **As new sheet** textbox and type the following: **Sunrise and Sunset**
52. Click the **Finish** button.

53. The **Sunrise and Sunset** chart now appears on its own worksheet in your workbook.
54. Save your work.
55. Print the chart.
56. To display the daylight hours in a column chart, select (highlight) cells **D2 through D6**.
57. Click the **Chart Wizard** button on the Standard toolbar.
58. At the **Chart Wizard – Step 1 of 4 – Chart Type** dialog box, click on the Standard Types tab to bring it to the forefront, if necessary.
59. At the **Chart type** menu, select **Column**.
60. At the **Chart sub-type** menu, select the **Clustered column with 3-D visual effect chart**—the first one in the second row.
61. Click the **Next** button to continue.
62. At the **Chart Wizard – Step 2 of 4 – Chart Source Data** dialog box, notice that the numbers displayed on the horizontal axis are 1, 2, 3, and more. In order to tell *Microsoft Excel* that you want the specific city names displayed, click on the Series tab to bring it to the forefront.
63. At the **Category (X) axis labels** command line, click on the tiny worksheet icon that you see at the end of the command line. When you click on the icon, you will jump to your worksheet.
64. Select (highlight) cells **A2 through A6**—the city names. When highlighting cells A2 through A6, you will see "marching ants" around the area you selected. You have just indicated to *Microsoft Excel* that these are the labels you want displayed on the horizontal axis of your chart.
65. On top of your worksheet you should see a narrow **Chart Wizard – Step 2 of 4 – Chart Source – Category (X)** . . . window. The command line now contains the information *Microsoft Excel* needs to change the labels on the horizontal axis. Click on the tiny worksheet icon that you see at the end of the command line. When you click on the icon, you jump back to the Chart Wizard.
66. Click **Next** to continue.
67. At the **Chart Wizard – Step 3 of 4 – Chart Options** dialog box, click on the **Titles** tab to bring it to the forefront, if necessary.
68. Click in the **Chart title** textbox and type the following: **Daylight Hours**
69. Click in the **Category (X) axis** textbox and type the following: **Cities and States**
70. Click in the **Value (Z) axis** command line and type the following: **Hours**
71. Click the **Legends** tab to bring it to the forefront.

72. Click **Show Legend** to deselect it. The legend disappears from the chart display.

73. Click the **Next** button to continue.

74. At the **Chart Wizard – Step 4 of 4 – Chart Location** dialog box, click **As new sheet**.

75. Click in the **As new sheet** textbox and type the following: **Daylight Hours**

76. Click the **Finish** button.

77. The **Daylight Hours** chart now appears on its own worksheet in your workbook.

78. Save your work.

79. Print the chart.

80. Exit *Microsoft Excel*.

Assessment

- Referring to the line chart, discuss with students that the difference between the sunrise and the sunset lines indicates the amount of daylight hours. Based upon this line chart, can your students identify the city that has the longest daylight hours? Can your students identify the city that has the shortest daylight hours?

- Referring to the column chart, have students explain their findings about the cities' daylight hours. Compare the findings displayed in this chart with the findings displayed in the line chart.

Extension

- Have students compare the sunrise and sunset times for international cities, including cities in the Northern Hemisphere and cities in the Southern Hemisphere.

Related CD Files

- **Sunrise and Sunset.xls** (a copy of the **Sunrise and Sunset** workbook file used in this student lesson)

- **Sunrise and Sunset Data Organizer.doc** (a copy of the **Sunrise and Sunset Data Organizer** referred to in this lesson—a *Microsoft Word* file)

Sunrise and Sunset Data		
City and State	**Sunrise**	**Sunset**
Las Cruces, NM	6:41 AM	5:04 PM
Hesperia, CA	6:27 AM	4:42 PM
Brockton, MA	6:40 AM	4:19 PM
Oklahoma City, OK	7:10 AM	5:21 PM
Fairbanks, AK	9:44 AM	3:29 PM

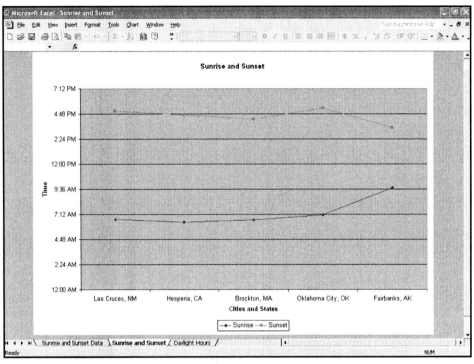

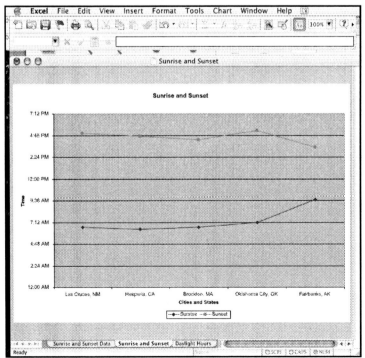

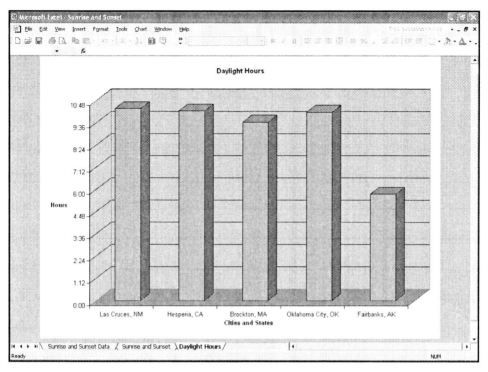

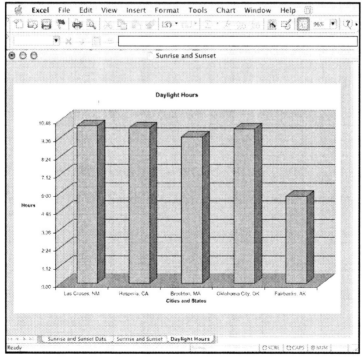

Sunrise and Sunset Data Organizer

City and State	Sunrise	Sunset

Sunrise and Sunset Data Organizer

City and State	Sunrise	Sunset

Sunrise and Sunset Data Organizer

City and State	Sunrise	Sunset

Seed Experiments
Grades 4 and Up

Lesson Summary

In this lesson, students plant seeds under two different conditions (cold and warm). They record the number of seeds germinated under each condition over time in a *Microsoft Excel* worksheet. Students create a chart that displays the differences between the germination rates.

Curriculum Concepts
- Germinating seeds
- Observing the affects of temperature on seed germination
- Collecting growth data
- Interpreting charts

Computer Skills
- Spreadsheet text entry
- Spreadsheet data entry
- Spreadsheet simple formatting
- Charting

Materials
- Two Petri dishes; small dishes with covers; or clear, plastic baggies
- Paper towels or filter paper
- Seeds (approximately 60 lentil or kidney bean seeds are recommended)
- Two classroom thermometers
- **Seed Data Collection Form**

Before the Computer
- In order to introduce the activity and foster discussion, ask students the following questions: Have you ever wondered what happens to a seed when it is placed in the ground? Do you think seeds grow quickly or slowly? Do you think weather has any effect on how seeds grow? This experiment will allow you to see what seeds do under ground and how temperature affects how they grow.

- In Explain to students that they will be planting seeds in two dishes. The first dish will be placed in a cool location and the second dish will be placed in a warm location. Students will observe and record data about the number of seeds germinating each day. They will put this data into a *Microsoft Excel* worksheet and create a chart that will help them compare the number of seeds that germinated under the two different conditions.

- In Help students place filter paper or a folded paper towel inside the dishes or bags. Have students moisten the paper until there is a tiny bit of standing water and place 30 seeds on top of the wet paper in each dish, spacing them as evenly as possible. Put the covers on the dishes or zip the baggies.

- In Place the first dish or bag of seeds in a warm place in the classroom. Place the second dish or bag of seeds in a cool place in the classroom. Place a thermometer next to each dish or bag of seeds and record the temperatures.

- In Have students use the **Seed Data Collection Form** for approximately three weeks, recording the date, time, number of seeds germinated, and temperatures. (The sample data was collected on Mondays, Wednesdays, and Fridays. The number of new seeds germinated was recorded.)

Note: If the paper dries out during this time, rewet it just a little. Don't leave excess water in the germination containers.

- In After the seeds have germinated, plant them in paper cups or in a garden.

At the Computer

1. Launch *Microsoft Excel.*
2. Click in cell **A1** and type the following: **Day**
3. Click in cell **A2** and type the following: **1**
4. Click in cell **A3** and enter the number of the next day you counted newly germinated seeds. (In our example, it was day **3**.)
5. Click in cell **A4** and enter the number of the next day you counted newly germinated seeds. (In our example, it was day **5**.)

6. Continue entering the numbers of the days you collected data in column A. (In our example, we entered the numbers of the days we collected data through cell **A10**.)

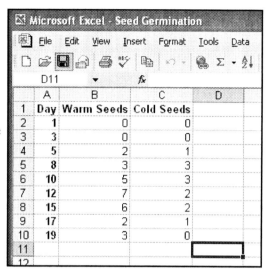

7. To format the row labels, click the **column heading A** to select (highlight) the entire column.

8. Click the **Bold** button on the Formatting toolbar.

9. While the column is still selected, adjust the column width. Click **Format** on the Menu bar.

10. Click **Column**.

11. Click **AutoFit Selection**.

12. Click in cell **B1** and type the following: **Warm Seeds**

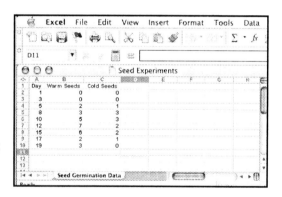

13. Click in cell **C1** and type the following: **Cold Seeds**

14. To format the column labels, click the **row heading 1** to select (highlight) the entire row.

15. Click the **Bold** button on the Formatting toolbar **twice**.

16. Click the **Center** button on the Formatting toolbar.

17. While the row is still selected, adjust the column widths. Click **Format** on the Menu bar.

18. Click **Column**.
19. Click **AutoFit Selection**.
20. Click in cell **B2** and enter the number of seeds germinated in the warm dish on the first day.
21. Click in cell **B3** and enter the number of seeds germinated in the warm dish on the second day you recorded data.
22. Continue in this manner until you have entered the number of seeds germinated in the warm dish each day during your investigation.
23. Click in cell **C2** and enter the number of seeds germinated in the cold dish on the first day.
24. Click in cell **C3** and enter the number of seeds germinated in the cold dish on the second day you recorded data.
25. Continue in this manner until you have entered the number of seeds germinated in the cold dish each day during your investigation.
26. Save your work.
27. To create a chart that displays the seed germination rates, select (highlight) the labels and values in the Warm Seeds and Cold Seeds columns. (In the sample spreadsheet, this is the range of cells from **B1 through C10**.)
28. Click on the **Chart Wizard** button on the standard toolbar.
29. At the **Chart Wizard – Step 1 of 4 – Chart Type** dialog box, click on the **Standard Types** tab to bring it to the forefront, if necessary.
30. At the **Chart type** menu, select **Line**.
31. At the **Chart sub-type** menu, select the **Line with markers displayed at each data value chart**—the first one in the second row.
32. Click the **Next** button to continue.
33. At the **Chart Wizard – Step 2 of 4 – Chart Source Data** dialog box, notice that the numbers displayed on the horizontal axis are 1, 2, 3, 4, 5, 6, etc. They do not reflect the specific days you recorded in the Day column (1, 3, 5, 8, 10, 12, 15, 17, 19). In order to "tell" *Microsoft Excel* you want the specific days recorded in the Day column on the horizontal access, click on the **Series** tab to bring it to the forefront.
34. At the **Category (X) axis labels** command line, click on the tiny worksheet icon that you see at the end of the command line. When you click on the icon, you will jump to your worksheet.
35. Select (highlight) the values in the Day column. Do not select the column label. You have just indicated to *Microsoft Excel* that these are the numbers that you want displayed on the horizontal axis.

36. At the top of your worksheet you should see a narrow **Chart Wizard – Step 2 of 4 – Chart Source Data – Category (X)** . . . window. The command line now contains the information *Microsoft Excel* needs to change the numbering on the horizontal axis. Click on the tiny worksheet icon that you see at the end of the command line. When you click on the icon, you will jump back to the Chart Wizard.

37. When you return to Source Data dialog box, click the **Next** button to continue.

38. At the **Chart Wizard – Step 3 of 4 – Chart Options** dialog box, click on the **Titles** tab to bring it to the forefront, if necessary.

39. Click in the **Chart title** textbox and type the following: **Seed Germination**

40. Click in the **Category (X) axis** textbox and type the following: **Days**

41. Click in the **Value (Y) axis** textbox and type the following: **Number of Seeds Germinated**

42. Click the **Legend** tab to bring it to the forefront.

43. Under **Placement**, click **Bottom**.

44. Click the **Next** button to continue.

45. At the **Chart Wizard – Step 4 of 4 – Chart Location** dialog box, click **As new sheet**.

46. Click in the **As new sheet** textbox and type the following: **Seed Germination**

47. Click the **Finish** button.

48. The **Seed Germination** chart now appears on its own worksheet in your workbook.

49. Save your work.

50. Print the chart.

51. Exit *Microsoft Excel*.

Assessment

- Using the **Seed Germination** worksheet and chart as references, have the class discuss the seed experiment and answer the following questions:
    1. How does the temperature seem to affect the seeds?
    2. Knowing this, how might the weather affect seeds and crops?
    3. What might happen if the temperature suddenly changed in one or both locations?
    4. How long did it take the first seed to germinate?

Extension

- Create a seed germination bulletin board that displays a sample **Seed Collection Data Form, Seed Germination** worksheet and chart, and sketches representing each step of the investigation.

- Return to the **Seed Germination** worksheet and complete additional calculations, such as the total number of seeds germinated under each condition (using the AutoSum feature).

- Have students enter the temperature data into the **Seed Germination** worksheet as well. Create charts displaying the relationship between the temperature recorded and the number of seeds germinated.

Related CD Files

- **Seed Germination.xls** (a copy of the Seed Germination workbook used in this student lesson)

- **Seed Data Collection Form.doc** (a copy of the **Seed Data Collection Form** referred to in this lesson—a *Microsoft Word* file)

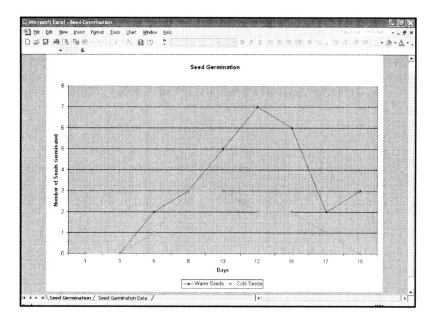

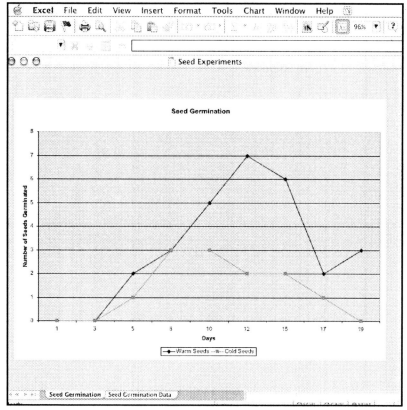

Seed Data Collection Form

Directions: Use this form to help you collect data about seed germination rates. First, fill out the Day One Information. Then fill out the Every Day Information each weekday you are in class or as directed by your teacher. Skip or cross out those days, such as weekends, that you do not record any germination rate data.

Day One Information

Date seeds were placed in containers	
Time seeds were placed in containers	
Types of seeds you are using	
Number of seeds in each container	
Location of the first container	
Temperature at the first location	
Location of the second container	
Temperature at the second location	

Every Day Information

Day	Date	Time	Seeds Germinated in the Warm Location	Temperature in the Warm Location	Seeds Germinated in the Cold Location	Temperature in the Cold Location
1			0		0	
2						
3						
4						
5						
6						
7						
8						
9						
10						
11						
12						
13						
14						
15						
16						
17						
18						
19						
20						
21						

Soil Analysis
Grades 4-8

Lesson Summary

In this lesson, students create soil shakes and analyze the layers of different kinds of soil that result from mixing water and dirt. Students measure the soil layers in both centimeters and inches, making this an ideal science/mathematics lesson.

Curriculum Content

- Analyzing soil composition
- Measuring in metric units
- Converting metric to standard units

Computer Skills

- Spreadsheet text entry
- Spreadsheet data entry
- Spreadsheet simple formatting
- Spreadsheet simple formulas
- Charting

Materials

- Soil samples from one or more locations in your area
- Jars that can be filled with water and soil and shaken
- Rulers that measure in inches and centimeters

Before the Computer

- Provide students with a variety of soil and water mixtures (moist soil). Allow them to look at, feel, smell, and compare the soil and water mixtures. Have students note what they see in the mixtures (such as sand, clay, etc.).
- Have students find out what makes good soil for planting in a garden. (FYI: The composition is 40 percent sand, 40 percent silt, and 20 percent clay)

- Help students create soil shakes. Have each student fill a jar 2/3 full with water. The each student should add enough soil to fill the jar to just below the rim.

- Allow students to label and shake their jars. Then place the jars in a safe place to sit over night.

- On the following day, students should be able to see distinct layers of soil forming in their jars. Have them draw or sketch the jars and their contents, labeling and describing the different layers.

- Using a ruler with centimeters, have students identify and measure each layer within the soil shake, as well as the total amount of soil.

At the Computer

1. Launch *Microsoft Excel*.
2. Click in cell **A1** and type the following: **Soil Composition**
3. Click in cell **A2** and type the following: **Organic Material**
4. Click in cell **A3** and type the following: **Suspended Clay**
5. Click in cell **A4** and type the following: **Clay**
6. Click in cell **A5** and type the following: **Silt**
7. Click in cell **A6** and type the following: **Sand**
8. To format the row labels, click the **column heading A** to select (highlight) the entire row.
9. Click the **Bold** button on the Formatting toolbar.
10. While the entire column is still selected, adjust the column width. Click **Format** on the Menu bar.
11. Click **Column**.
12. Click **AutoFit Selection**.
13. Click in cell **B1** and type the following: **Centimeters**
14. Click in cell **B2** and type the following: **Inches**
15. To format the column headings, click the **row heading 1** to select (highlight) the entire row.
16. Click the **Bold** button on the Formatting toolbar twice.
17. Click the **Center** button on the Formatting toolbar.
18. While the entire row is still selected, adjust the column widths. Click **Format** on the Menu bar.
19. Click **Column**.
20. Click **AutoFit Selection**.

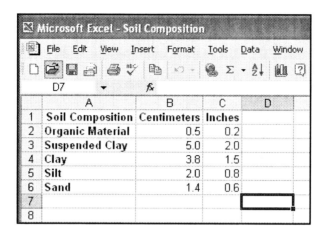

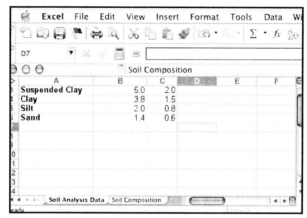

21. Finally, format the Centimeters and Inches columns to display one place after the decimal point. Click the **column heading B** to select (highlight) the entire column.

22. Hold down the **Control** key on your keyboard and click the **column heading C** to select (highlight) the entire column as well.

23. Click **Format** on the Menu bar.

24. Click **Cells**.

25. At the **Format Cells** dialog box, click the **Numbers** tab to bring it to the forefront, if necessary.

26. Under **Category**, click **Number**.
27. In the **Decimal places** textbox, type the following: **1**
28. Click **OK**.
29. Click in cell **B2** and enter the measurement (in centimeters) of the organic material in the soil shake jar.
30. Click in cell **B3** and enter the measurement (in centimeters) of the suspended clay in the soil shake jar.
31. Click in cell **B4** and enter the measurement (in centimeters) of the clay in the soil shake jar.
32. Click in cell **B5** and enter the measurement (in centimeters) of the silt in the soil shake jar.
33. Click in cell **B6** and enter the measurement (in centimeters) of the sand in the soil shake jar.
34. Save your work.
35. Rather than measuring again in inches, students can covert metric to standard measurements using a simple formula. Click in cell **C2** and type the following formula: **=B2*0.3937**
36. Click on the **Enter** button to the left of the formula bar.
37. Use the **AutoFill feature** to copy the conversion formula from cell **C2 through cell C7**.
38. Save your work.
39. To create a pie chart that displays the soil composition in centimeters, select (highlight) cells **A1 through B6**.
    Click the **Chart Wizard** button on the Standard toolbar.
40. At the **Chart Wizard – Step 1 of 4 – Chart Type** dialog box, click the **Standard Types** tab to bring it to the forefront, if necessary.
41. At the **Chart type** menu, select **Pie**.
42. At the **Chart sub-type** menu, select the **Exploded Pie chart**—the first one in the second row.
43. Click the **Next** button to continue.
44. At the **Chart Wizard – Step 2 of 4 – Chart Source Data** dialog box, click **Next** to continue.
45. At the **Chart Wizard – Step 3 of 4 – Chart Options** dialog box, click on the **Titles** tab to bring it to the forefront, if necessary.
46. Click in the **Chart title** textbox and type the following: **Soil Composition**
47. Click the **Data Labels** tab to bring it to the forefront.
48. Under the **Label Contains** menu, select **Category name**.
49. Also select **Percentage**.

50. Click **Next** to continue.

51. At the **Chart Wizard – Step 4 of 4 – Chart Location** dialog box, select **As new sheet**.

52. Click in the **As new sheet** textbox and type the following: Soil Composition

53. Click the **Finish** button.

54. The **Soil Composition** chart now appears on its own worksheet in your workbook.

55. Save your work.

56. Print the chart.

57. Exit *Microsoft Excel*.

Assessment

- Student pie charts should display the percents for each soil type and add up to 100 percent.

Extension

- Have students create another pie chart using inches rather than centimeters. Compare the two charts. They should be identical.

- Have students collect soil samples from two different locations in their area. Have them complete the same measurements and calculations on the two new samples. They can then compare the different soil compositions from the two different locations.

Related CD Files

- **Soil Analysis.xls** (a copy of the Soil Analysis workbook used in this student lesson)

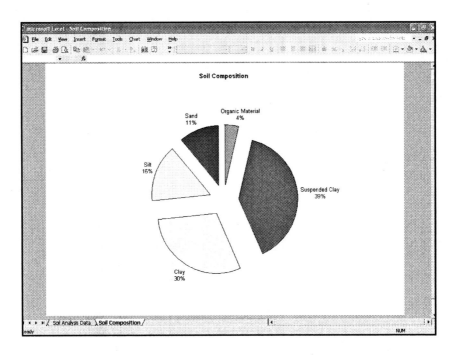

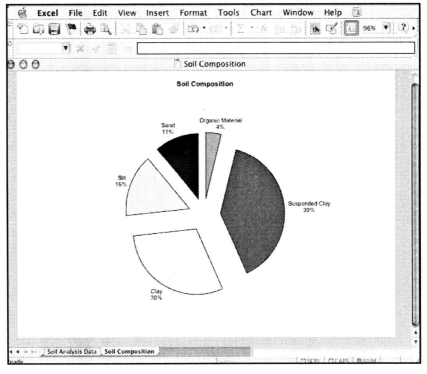

Planets—Weighty Matters
Grades 4-8

Lesson Summary

Want to lose weight? Just move to Mercury, Mars, or Pluto. In this lesson, students discover how much they weigh on the moon, on Jupiter, and on the other planets in our solar system. Using a *Microsoft Excel* workbook, students enter their names and Earth weights. *Microsoft Excel* automatically calculates their weights on all the planets in our solar system. Students can also compare the weights of other people and objects.

Curriculum Concepts

- Explain mass
- Explain weight
- Explain the force of gravity and its relationship to mass and weight
- Discover the affects of mass and gravity on weight on other planets

Computer Skills

- Spreadsheet text entry
- Spreadsheet data entry
- Charting
- Interpreting chart display

Materials

- **Weight on Planets** file

Before the Computer

- Discuss with students the difference between mass and weight. Be sure to stress that weight depends on the force of gravity, whereas mass does not.
- After discussing the concept of gravity, have students guess how much they might weight on different planets.

At the Computer

1. Launch *Microsoft Excel*.

2. Insert the **Excel for Terrified Teachers CD** in the CD-ROM drive of your computer system.

3. Click **File** on the Menu bar.

4. Click **Open**.

5. At the **Open** window, click the **Look in** list arrow and navigate to the CD-ROM drive of your computer system.

6. From the list of files on the CD-ROM drive, click **Weight on Planets**.

7. Click the **Open** button.

8. Save the file onto your computer system.

9. Click in cell **A5** and type a student's name, replacing **Student 1**, such as **Keith Ray**.

10. Click in cell **B5** and type in the student's weight, such as **90**.

11. Then click in cell **A6**. Notice that your student's weight on the moon and all the planets in our solar system are automatically calculated.

12. Continue entering students' names in column A and their weights in column B.

13. Save your work.

14. To chart an individual student's weight on all the planets, click on the **row heading 1** to select (highlight) the entire row.

15. Hold down the **Control key** on your keyboard and click on the row heading 5 to select (highlight) the entire row. Rows 1 and 5 (or the row you selected) should now be selected (highlighted).

16. Click the **Chart Wizard** button on the **Standard** toolbar.

17. At the **Chart Wizard – Step 1 of 4 – Chart Type** dialog box, click the **Standard Types** tab to bring it to the forefront, if necessary.

18. At the **Chart type** menu, select **Column**.

19. At the **Chart sub-type** menu, select the **Clustered column chart**—the first one in the first row.

20. Click the **Next** button to continue.

21. At the **Chart Wizard – Step 2 of 4 – Chart Source Data** dialog box, click **Next** to continue.

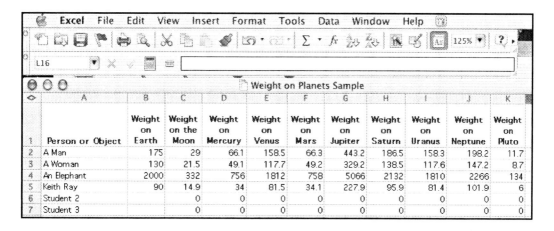

22. At the **Chart Wizard – Step 3 of 4 – Chart Options** dialog box, click the **Titles** tab to bring it to the forefront, if necessary.

23. In the Chart title textbox type the following: **My Weight on the Earth, Moon, and Other Planets**.

Note: Instead of using the word My, feel free to substitute the student's actual name.

24. In the **Value (Y) axis** textbox and type the following: **Pounds**

25. Click on the **Legends** tab to bring it to the forefront.

26. Click in the **Show Legend** box to deselect it and remove the legend from your display.

27. Click on the **Data Labels** tab to bring it to the forefront.

28. Under the **Label Contains** menu, select **Value**.

29. Click the **Next** button to continue.

30. At the **Chart Wizard – Step 4 of 4 – Chart Location** dialog box, click **As new sheet**.

31. Click in the **As new sheet** textbox and type the following: **My Weight— Keith Ray**

Note: Substitute your student's actual name, especially if you will be saving one chart for each student.

32. Click the **Finish** button.

33. The **My Weight—Keith Ray** chart now appears on its own worksheet in your workbook.

34. Save your work.

35. Print the chart to share with your student.

36. Save the workbook file.

37. Continue charting the next student's weight or exit *Microsoft Excel*.

Assessment

- Have students compare/contrast their weights on different planets.
- Have students consider the relationship among the sun, a planet's size, a planet's weight and how much students weigh there.
- Have students identify planets where they would be lighter and heavier than on Earth. Ask if students would be light as a feather on any of the plants. Ask if students would be heavier than a whale on any of the planets.

Extension

- Have students form groups to research one of the nine planets and present information to the class on size, composition, distance from sun, distance from the earth, etc. All of this information can be entered into a Microsoft Excel worksheet.

Related CD Files

- **Weight on Planets.xls** (a copy of the **Weight on Planets** file used to begin this student lesson)
- **Weight on Planets Sample.xls** (a copy of the **Weight on Planets Sample** file displayed in this lesson)

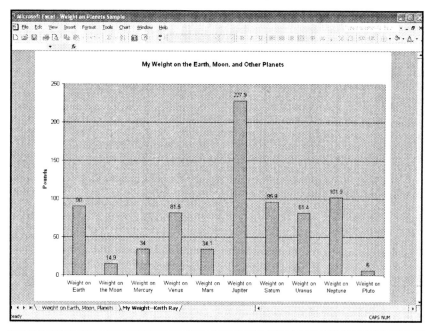

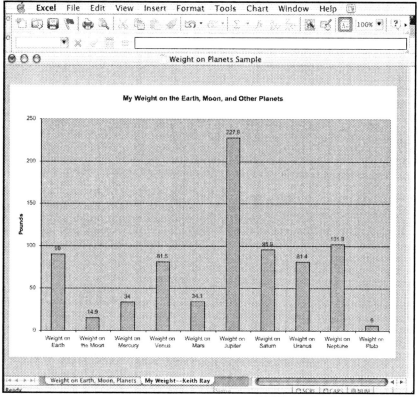

Glossary

Absolute cell references—Cell references within a formula that do not adjust when copied from one cell to another. The dollar sign is used to specify absolute cell references.

Active cell—The cell in your worksheet that has been selected. The active cell has a bolder gridline around it. The active cell's address appears in the Name Box above the worksheet.

AutoFill—A *Microsoft Excel* feature that allows you to quickly apply the contents of one cell to another cell or a range of selected cells.

AutoSum—A *Microsoft Excel* function that automatically identifies and adds ranges of cells in your worksheet.

Button—A clickable "hot spot" on your screen. Clicking a button initiates an action in *Microsoft Excel*, such as save or print.

Cancel button—A button to the left of the formula bar that allows you to cancel the contents of the active cell.

CD-ROM—Compact disc-read only memory stores files in digital form. It can be accessed to open files just like your floppy disk drive and hard drive.

CD-ROM drive—The mechanism used to access files on your CD-ROM. The CDROM drive is typically designated as drive D:\ on your computer system.

Cell—The rectangular-shaped area on a worksheet that is created by the intersection of a column and a row. The cell is where you enter and store data in a worksheet.

Cell address—The name of a cell that is determined by the intersection of a column and a row. The address of the cell that is formed by the intersection of column A and row 8 is A8.

Cell grid—The lines on your worksheet that separate the columns and rows.

Click—The action you perform when you push a button on the mouse to position your cursor, select an item, or activate a *Microsoft Excel* feature.

Close—A drop down menu item that puts away a workbook file you are no longer using.

Close button—The small square button with the X in it at the top of your screen. Clicking on this button closes the *Microsoft Excel* program.

Close window button— The small square button with the X in it at the end of the menu bar. It is identical to and located just below the close button. Clicking on this button closes the workbook you are no longer using.

Column—In a worksheet, the vertical spaces with headings A, B, C, and so on.

Command line—A place in a *Microsoft Excel* window where you type information, such as a file name.

Copy—The process of selecting numbers and/or text and placing them in memory for pasting in another location. When you copy, the original numbers and/or text you selected remains on the screen.

Cursor —The symbol displayed on the computer screen (a blinking bar, an I-beam, an arrowhead, or other icon) that indicates where your next keystroke will appear in your worksheet.

Cut—To remove text or numbers from the active cell or range of selected cells in a worksheet.

Default—How the settings are automatically. For example, the default column width in a *Microsoft Excel* worksheet is 8.43 points.

Delete—To remove text or numbers from the active cell or range of selected cells in a worksheet.

Delete key—A key on your keyboard that erases items on your screen. When you press the delete key, the text or numbers to the right of the cursor are cleared. If text or numbers in a cell or range of cells is selected, when you press the delete key, the entire highlighted area is cleared.

Dialog box—A box that appears on your screen that prompts you to provide some type of input, such as text or values, or that prompts you to make a selection or click a button.

Deselect—After a range of cells has been selected (highlighted) and worked with, clicking in an unselected area of the worksheet to deactivate the original selection or highlighting.

Drag—When you move the mouse while holding down the mouse button (usually the left) to select a range of cells.

Enter key—A key on your keyboard that you press when you want your cursor to move the next line. Pressing enter also indicates that you have made a selection or accepted a formula. It is the same as the Return key.

Enter button—A button to the left of the formula bar that you click to accept the contents of the active cell, such as a formula.

Exit—A drop-down menu item that allows you to quite the *Microsoft Excel* program when selected.

File—A document that is stored on your computer, floppy diskette, or CD-ROM. In *Microsoft Excel*, a file is also known as a workbook.

Filename—The name you give a file upon saving it.

Fill down—A *Microsoft Excel* feature that allows you to copy information in an active cell to another cell or range of cells you have selected vertically.

Fill right—A *Microsoft Excel* feature that allow you to copy information in an active cell to another cell or range of cells you have selected horizontally.

Floppy disk drive— The mechanism used to access files on your floppy diskette. The floppy disk drive is typically designated as drive A:\ on your computer system.

Font—The type face of letters formed as you enter text in your worksheet, such as Helvetica and Anal.

Formatting—Working with the attributes of components of the worksheet on your screen, such as resizing, bolding, and centering the text.

Formatting toolbar—A series of drop-down menus and buttons above your worksheet that allows you change the type face, type size, type attributes, text and number alignment, and more.

Formula—A combination of numbers and symbols used to express a calculation. The formula =SUM(A] :A6) tells *Microsoft Excel* to add the numbers in cells Al through A6.

Formula bar—A command line above the worksheet where text, numbers, and formulas are entered into a worksheet.

Function—A drop-down menu item and a button on the standard toolbar that allows you to select a formula that you wish to apply to data in your worksheet.

Hard disk drive—A high-speed, high-density alternative to the floppy disk drive. So called because the platter on which the data is stored is rigid.

Hardware—The parts of your computer that you can see and touch.

Headings—The identifying letters and numbers for columns and rows. Columns are identified by the letters A, B, C, and so on.   Rows are identified by the numbers 1, 2, 3, and so on.

Highlight—When the mouse is dragged over the cells in a worksheet, they become highlighted. The highlighting indicates that the cells are selected and ready to be manipulated.

Icon—A small image on your computer screen used to represent a specific program or to initiate an action in *Microsoft Excel.*

Input—Data that comes into the computer from some kind of input device such as a disk drive, the keyboard, or a microphone.

Insert—To enter text or numbers at the position of the cursor or cell pointer.

Internet—An international web of computer networks.

Justification—Alignment of text or numbers within a worksheet cell. The alignment may be left-justified, centered, or right-justified.

Label—The identifying name that reflects the information contained in a column or row in a worksheet. A column label may be Name. A row label may be Date.

Landscape—A screen orientation where the longer side of a worksheet or chart extends from side to side. For typical documents landscape orientation is typically 11' x 8.5. It is the opposite of portrait orientation which is 8.5" x 11".

Launch—To open a software program, such as *Microsoft Excel*, so you can use it.

Legend—An explanation of the data series within a chart.

Menu bar—The set of menu items, such as File, Edit, View, Insert, etc., displayed at the top of the screen in *Microsoft Excel.*

Monitor—The screen you use to display the *Microsoft Excel* worksheet that is being processed by your computer.

Mouse—A small, mechanical piece of computer hardware that you roll on your desk and click to control where text and numbers will be placed in your worksheet, as well as which items are selected on your screen.

Mouse button—One of two or three spots on the mouse that you depress or click to make a selection.

Name box—A display area above your worksheet that shows the cell address of the active cell or range of cells.

New—A drop-down menu item and a button on the standard toolbar that allows you to open a new workbook file.

Open—A drop-down menu item and a button on the standard toolbar that allows you to open an existing workbook file.

Paste—To insert text or numbers that were selected and copied into an active cell or range of cells.

Pointer arrow—The arrow that appears on the screen and moves when the mouse is moved.

Portrait orientation—A screen orientation where the shorter side of a worksheet or chart extends from side to side. For typical documents portrait orientation is 8.5" x 11'. It is the opposite of landscape orientation which is 11" x 8.5".

Print—To make a hard copy of a worksheet or other document.

Printer—The device you use for producing a hard copy of your *Microsoft Excel* worksheet.

Relative cell references—Cell references within a formula that adjust when copied from one cell to another.

Return key— A key on your keyboard that you press when you want your cursor to move the next line. Pressing return also indicates that you have made a selection or accepted a formula. It is the same as the Enter key.

Rows—In a worksheet, the horizontal spaces with the headings 1, 2, 3, and so on.

Save—The pull-down menu item or button on the standard toolbar that allows you to store your workbook on the hard drive or your floppy diskette.

Select—Identifying a cell or range of cells so that you can apply some type of action, such as copy, delete, or bold.

Sheet tabs—Tabs you see at the bottom of your workbook file. The tabs are labeled Sheet1, Sheet2, Sheet3, and so on, although you can rename the tabs, giving them more meaningful names. They represent the worksheets within the workbook.

Shift/Tab—A key combination on your keyboard that allows you to move the active cell to the left.

Spreadsheet—An application program, such as *Microsoft Excel,* that appears as a ledger and allows you to enter text and numerical data in rows and columns

Standard toolbar— A series of drop-down menus and buttons above your worksheet that allows you open, save, print, and preview workbook files. It also allows you to quickly cut, copy, and paste selected areas of your worksheet and more.

Tab key—A navigation key on your keyboard that allows you to move your active cell one cell to the right.

Template—A way to save a workbook file so that you can use its structure over and over again. When you create or open a template file, always rename it so that the original file remains intact.

Text—The letters or words that you type into a cell in a *Microsoft Excel* worksheet.

Window—An enclosed area on your screen that is an independent object for data-processing purposes. Several windows can be open at the same time, enable you to easily switch from one task to another.

Word processing program—A productivity software application used primarily for working with written communication, such as text.

Word wrap—A characteristic of the *Microsoft Excel* program that allows text that extends beyond the right side of the cell to move to the beginning of a new line within the cell.

Workbook—A *Microsoft Excel* file that contains individual worksheets. It is also sometimes called a spreadsheet file.

Worksheet—A "page" within a *Microsoft Excel* workbook that contains columns, rows, and cells.

CD-ROM File Names

Page	Activity/Lesson Name	File Name
29	Activity 4—Saving, Using, and Renaming a Workbook Template	Learning Center Schedule.xls
29	Activity 4—Saving, Using, and Renaming a Workbook Template	Learning Center January.xls
46	Activity 8—Changing the Text Color	Reading Progress.xls
49	Activity 9—Selecting, Copying, and Pasting Data	Reading Progress.xls
57	Activity 10—Using the Fill-Down and Fill-Right Features	Reading Progress.xls
63	Activity 11—Setting Horizontal and Vertical Split Lines	Reading Progress Data.xls
70	Activity 12—Using the AutoSum Feature	Reading Progress Data.xls
73	Activity 13—Using the AutoFill to Extend Formulas	Reading Progress Data.xls
73	Activity 13—Using the AutoFill to Extend Formulas	Reading Progress Totals.xls
78	Activity 14—Previewing and Improving the Worksheet	Reading Progress Totals.xls
78	Activity 14—Previewing and Improving the Worksheet	Number of Books Read.xls
87	Activity 15—Centering and Setting the Print Area	Number of Books Read.xls
87	Activity 15—Centering and Setting the Print Area	Number of Books Read Final.xls
94	Activity 16—Using Chart Wizard to Create a Column Chart	Number of Books Read Final.xls
94	Activity 16—Using Chart Wizard to Create a Column Chart	Number of Books Read Chart.xls
107	Activity 17—Renaming, Moving, and Deleting Worksheets	Number of Books Read Chart.xls
107	Activity 17—Renaming, Moving, and Deleting Worksheets	Reading Data and Chart.xls
114	Activity 18—Adding a Worksheet to a Workbook	Reading Data and Chart.xls
114	Activity 18—Adding a Worksheet to a Workbook	Reading Data with Wksht.xls
122	Activity 19—Creating a Line Chart with a Data Table	Reading Data with Wksht.xls
122	Activity 19—Creating a Line Chart with a Data Table	Reading Data with Prin Chart.xls
134	Activity 20—Adding a Background Picture to a Chart	Reading Data with Prin Chart.xls
134	Activity 20—Adding a Background Picture to a Chart	Reading Data with Prin Line.xls

CD-ROM File Names *(cont.)*

Page	Activity/Lesson Name	File Name
134	Activity 20—Adding a Background Picture to a Chart	Book.tiff
142	Activity 21—Integrating a Microsoft Excel Chart	Reading Data with Prin Line.xls
142	Activity 21—Integrating a Microsoft Excel Chart	Reading Progress Memo.doc
142	Activity 21—Integrating a Microsoft Excel Chart	Reading Progress Chart.doc
151	Activity 22—Creating a Pie Chart	Pizza Data and Chart.xls
159	Activity 23—Using Relative and Absolute Formulas	Gradebook Template.xls
171	Activity 24—Using the Gradebook	Gradebook Template.xls
171	Activity 24—Using the Gradebook	Gradebook First Nine Weeks.xls
177	If You . . . Book Favorites	If You . . . .xls
182	Pets Galore	Pets Galore.xls
182	Pets Galore	Pets Galore Data Org.doc
191	Author Awards	Story Elements.xls
197	Actors and Animals	Actors and Animals.xls
197	Actors and Animals	Actors and Animals Tally.doc
204	Guess and Test	Guess and Test.xls
210	Best Meal Deal	Best Meal Deal.xls
210	Best Meal Deal	Best Meal Deal Data Org.doc
217	Puppy Play Area	Puppy Play Area.xls
217	Puppy Play Area	Puppy Play Area Data Org.xls
225	Currency Conversions	Currency Conversions.xls
225	Currency Conversions	Travel Mates Fact Finder.doc
225	Currency Conversions	Currency Exchange Rates.xls
234	Presidential Parade	Presidential Parade.xls

CD-ROM File Names *(cont.)*

Page	Activity/Lesson Name	File Name
234	Presidential Parade	Presidential Data Org.doc
234	Presidential Parade	Presidential Data Org Sample.doc
242	Population Explosion	Population Explosion.xls
242	Population Explosion	Population Explosion Sample.xls
242	Population Explosion	Population Data Org.doc
253	Weekend Watch	Weekend Watch.xls
253	Weekend Watch	Weekend Television Log.doc
260	High Mountains and Low Valleys	Mountains and Valleys.xls
260	High Mountains and Low Valleys	High and Low Assess.doc
260	High Mountains and Low Valleys	High and Low Data Org.doc
269	Sunrise and Sunset	Sunrise and Sunset.xls
269	Sunrise and Sunset	Sunrise and Sunset Data Org.doc
279	Seed Experiments	Seed Experiments.xls
279	Seed Experiments	Seed Data Collection.doc
287	Soil Analysis	Soil Composition.xls
293	Planets—Weighty Matters	Weight on Planets.xls
293	Planets—Weighty Matters	Weight on Planets Sample.xls